CONTENTS

PART 3: TAOISM IN THE CHINESE ART OF GUNG FU

PART 4: IDEAS AND OPINIONS

APPENDICES

"Although Bruce Lee had many students in many locations throughout his lifetime, while in Seattle he was fortunate to have had several who thoroughly digested his teachings and have taken great pains to do their part in preserving them. Foremost among these individuals is Taky Kimura, whom Bruce entrusted to run his Seattle school and who has remained faithful to both Bruce and Bruce's teachings for over 37 years. The author also wishes to acknowledge the contribution made by Jesse Glover, who was Bruce's first student in America, and himself an author of several excellent books on Bruce's early years in Seattle. Additional thanks are due to Fred Sato, Ed Hart, Skip Ellsworth, and Doug Palmer, who have all given freely of their time in sharing their recollections of Bruce and his art during this fascinating period of his development."

DEDICATION

To Taky Kimura: A man who has proven himself loyal and true to the wishes and interests of his friend and sifu, Bruce Lee, over a period of many years. A man who has never once attempted to exploit the depth of his relationship with Bruce Lee, no matter how tough times got. A man who has always placed principle above commerce, decency above profit, friendship above fame, genuineness above ego, humbleness above position, harmony above title, and love above all. Bruce Lee picked his friends according to their character, and he never committed to paper words that weren't first committed to his heart. And, to this end, he once wrote: "To Taky, whose ability I respect and friendship I treasure." It is with the profoundest gratitude for all he has done for Bruce Lee and his family, and the profoundest respect for the manner in which he has done it, that this book is dedicated to Taky Kimura.

In Pursuit of
a Passion

By Linda Lee Cadwell

In 1963, a 23-year-old student at the University of Washington was invited to give a guest lecture on Chinese philosophy at Garfield High School where I was in my senior year. This was to be my first knowledge of Bruce Lee—a student of philosophy who happened also to be a teacher of gung fu. When the name "Bruce Lee" is mentioned, most of the world envisions a superhuman action star of martial art mayhem, but my quintessential memory of him is as a thinker, an eternal scholar, and an explorer in search of his soul. Via the medium of film, by sheer force of his personality, Bruce communicated a strong message of strength, power, and charisma, but in these hither-to-private papers you will be introduced to Bruce Lee, the student of life, the designer of his destiny.

The philosophy of martial art was Bruce's passion. It was out of this love for wisdom that Bruce gave himself the freedom to create his personal philosophy for living. But before he could be free to take that journey, he had to pack his bag with the tools he would need along the way. Formal schooling and gung fu training were the first tools, followed by years of self-education through books and research. The essays in this volume were written when Bruce was in his early twenties—he is in the process of adding the tools to his bag which, as he evolved toward greater emergence of self, would become part of his being, thus freeing him from toting the extra baggage.

In martial art circles it is well known that Bruce was iconoclastic in his ideas about the practice and application of traditional styles. Initially regarded as a young upstart shooting his mouth off about customs that were rooted in thousands of years of history, it did not take long for the martial art community to realize that this was a wise-beyond-his-years young man who wore his self-confidence as comfortably as a suit of clothes. Bruce's "radical" ideas were not delivered off the cuff, but were, in fact, the product of many years of study and a deep-rooted knowledge of the very things to which he often objected. To be effective in his arguments against the restrictions imposed by *clinging* to certain traditional martial art practices, it was first necessary for Bruce to gain a thorough understanding of the *roots* of these traditions. To his mind there was no unconditional acceptance of styles, forms, or rigid thought patterns, however it was only after he had achieved a high respect for the underlying principles of traditional ideas in martial art that he was able to free himself from being bound by the chains of unreasoned beliefs. Respecting some traditions as beneficial, rejecting others as stifling to personal development, Bruce was then free to liberate his own ideas, to expand his consciousness, to enter fully into his process of becoming a true artist of the martial way and a real human being.

The ideas on these pages are among the earliest written records of Bruce's journey into the realm of philosophical wisdom. In writing his interpretation of principles that have come down through the ages, he was able to apply them, first to his way of gung fu, and to his way of life as well. The yin/yang symbol, for instance, which is so popularly used nowadays, *without understanding,* to indicate anything of Asian or mystic origin, held tremendous significance for Bruce. He explains in these essays how it forms the basis for gung fu theory and in fact for the Taoist interpretation of the Universe. It is one thing to understand a principle intellectually, but Bruce was able to apply yin/yang theory to combative technique, as well as to the understanding of the relationship between man and woman.

Immersing himself in the study of ancient wisdom was the essential step for Bruce to arrive at that crucial point of introspection from where he was able to discern the principles that were essential for his own growth. Insight is not a quality that comes naturally, rather it is a characteristic that is nurtured through intelligent decision-making. It was through the process of applying his intelligence that Bruce developed deep insights into living the *Tao of gung fu.* He made passionate inquiry into every aspect of living the martial way, he respected traditional beliefs, but was not bound by unexamined tradition, he created his own philosophical outlook on life, and lived it and breathed it every moment of every day—this was Bruce's process. In this volume, he shares that process with you.

It is a blessing to have a passion in life. Bruce was blessed in that regard as are we, the beneficiaries of his passion.

PREFACE

By John Little

In the year 1963, twenty-two-year-old Bruce Lee sat down to write a little ninety-seven page primer on the then little-known martial art of gung fu. The book was titled *Chinese Gung Fu: The Philosophical Art of Self Defense* (the only book that Lee ever authored during his lifetime, by the way). Even then, Lee had envisioned writing a bigger and more in-depth book on his beloved art, going so far as to write on page seven of that little book:

> *In the very near future, after my trip to the Orient, a more thorough book titled "The Tao of Chinese Gung Fu" will be published.*

By November of 1964, Lee was still working on the book, mentioning in a letter to a friend:

> *I'm in the process of completing a much [more] thorough book on the Tao of Gung Fu. . . . This book will contain my insight during these past five years. I've worked hard for it.*

This is that book. It was to have been published in 1965 and was intended by its author, Bruce Lee, to be his gift to the Western world.

While Lee scrapped the idea of publishing this book, he did not scrap his research notes or sample chapters. Lee left behind substantial chapter writings, notes, photographs, and research materials for books on both gung fu and his then newly created martial art of jeet kune do. In order to shed further light on Lee's own process of intellectual growth and development as a martial artist, these materials are now presented through an exclusive and exhaustive publishing project involving Tuttle Publishing and the Bruce Lee Estate. I am honored that Linda Lee Cadwell (Lee's widow) and Adrian Marshall (Lee's attorney) have selected me to be the one upon whose shoulders this giant and honored task has been placed.

To this end—and for this book particularly—I will ask you to forget about what you know or, more importantly, what you think you know about Chinese martial art. I want you to forget the term "jeet kune do" and any preconceptions you may have formed regarding it. When Bruce Lee sat down to write the chapters and notes that formed this particular book, it was 1964 and his mind-set was still very much influenced by the traditional Chinese masters of the past. I should mention in fairness that Lee was already "non-classical" in his own approach to martial art, but only inasmuch as he had already started to question the efficacy of many of the so-called Chinese "classical" arts. Nevertheless, even his own gung fu system would continue to be defined by a Taoist philosophy emphasizing truth, reality, and the way things actually are—as opposed to how we might wish them to be.

In editing Lee's materials, I have taken great pains not to alter any of his original writings. Wherever there existed a paucity of written information on a specific topic that Lee had intended to include in his book, I have consulted his many notes and audio records for direction, nomenclature, and intent. Whenever a great master has taken the time to write something down, it is assumed that it is significant and therefore not to be touched, "interpreted," or altered in any way. It is in this spirit that I have proceeded with this book—and all other Bruce Lee–related projects I'm involved in. In the case of adapting Lee's rough notes (which were often jotted down on airline stationary at 30,000 feet above the ground or while riding in cars), I have attempted to flesh out Lee's point-form notations while remaining true to the gist or thrust of Lee's point. All of the manuscript amendments and alterations have been run past the discerning eyes of not only Lee's students from this particular era, but also Linda Lee Cadwell, whose deep concern and passion for preserving the integrity of her husband's writings cannot be questioned. These writings cover a span of almost twelve years and, because Lee was constantly refining and reducing the core essentials of what would eventually become his art of jeet kune do, separating Lee's Seattle, Oakland, Los Angeles, and early and later Hong Kong writings on the martial way into their appropriate eras has made for quite a task. There are still those among Lee's students who do not wish for his methods, ideas, and opinions to be taught to others. They zealously guard what (in some instances) has proven to be some knowledge they happened to obtain first hand from Bruce Lee as if it were holy writ. However, in this author's opinion, such secrecy runs contrary to the philosophy of Bruce Lee—a man who fought all of his life for the right of persons, regardless of skin color or ethnic origins, to learn whatever they feel will benefit them. Additionally, such a guarded position only results in half-truths being propagated and valid questions raised that remain unanswered. This denies justice to the legacy of a great man and to his posterity—both blood and intellectual. As American philosopher and Pulitzer Prize–winner Will Durant once said in the preface to his book, *The Story of Philosophy:*

> Let us not, then, be ashamed of teaching people. Those jealous ones who would guard their knowledge from the world have only themselves to blame if their exclusiveness and their barbarous terminology have led the world to seek in books, in lectures, and in adult education, the instruction which they themselves have failed to give. Let them be grateful that their halting efforts are aided by amateurs who love life enough to let it humanize their teaching. Perhaps each kind of teacher can be of aid to the other: the cautious scholar to check our enthusiasm with accuracy, and the enthusiast to pour warmth and blood into the fruits of scholarship. Between us we might build up in America an audience fit to listen to geniuses, and therefore ready to produce them. We are all imperfect teachers, but we may be forgiven if we have advanced the matter a little, and have done our best. We announce the prologue, and retire; after us better players will come.

It is in this spirit that we now proceed.

FOREWORD

By Taky Kimura

Please allow me to express my appreciation for the opportunity John Little has given me to share a few words about my relationship with one of the world's great icons, Bruce Lee.

John and I have known each other for over a year, and I have come to respect his sincerity and enjoy his friendship more and more as time goes by. John, like many of us, has excitedly worshipped and inspired himself to become the best that he can be after having been exposed to the great Bruce Lee; confident yet humble, genuinely assertive but sensitive to others. It is my humble opinion (and no small task!) that John has dedicated his life to researching, presenting, and, where necessary, extrapolating—in the most sincere manner—that which Bruce has left us in his many volumes of writings and private notes, so that we may all come to understand and share in Bruce's art and philosophy.

Bruce Lee was a multitalented person even at the age of eighteen as he brightened the horizons of Seattle. His five-foot-seven-inch frame would explode upon any given stage with the awesomeness of a comet and you were immediately captivated by his lovable personality. Bruce once shared with me the sentiment that he was relaxed and comfortable with people from all strata of society. He attributed this to the ultimate essence of the physicality and spirituality of the highest level of martial art. In my opinion, this was imbued in him, and Bruce lived and died the life of a true warrior.

I have often said that my first introduction to Bruce was an awesome experience. However I was also fortunate in being able to experience the many other aspects of his personality, such as the teenage comedian and the mature philosopher. I felt particularly enchanted by this last characteristic and somehow knew that I had to follow him.

For those unfamiliar with the background of Bruce Lee—the man who would in time come to write the book you are now holding in your hands—it may help if I take a moment to share with you how he came to introduce gung fu, a uniquely Chinese art, to North America. Bruce arrived in Seattle in 1959 at the age of eighteen, after a brief sojourn in San Francisco. With the help of several local television appearances and public demonstrations, Bruce began to give instruction to all Americans—regardless of race, creed, or national origin.

Even while growing up in Hong Kong, Bruce had experienced his fair share of prejudice and discrimination. This led him to become involved in the martial arts for both mental and physical self-preservation. He often spoke to me of the way the British officers looked down upon and mistreated the Chinese. From this background, Bruce swore to use the martial arts as a tool to express his ultimate desire: to create equality among the peoples of the world.

Even in Seattle during this early stage of his life's journey, Bruce denounced the "classical mess" and promoted the art of simplicity and harmony. In time, Bruce would modify his vast knowledge of the many arts to arrive at the ultimate stage of realistic simplicity: jeet kune do. However, whether he was instructing his students in the Jun Fan method of gung fu or in jeet kune do, Bruce understood that in either case, simplicity, honesty, and desire comes only from deep within your heart, and he incorporated this precious characteristic into all of his teachings.

Bruce was uniquely possessed with natural-born attributes: speed, coordination, gracefulness, high mentality, and charm. All of these factors contributed to his keen sense of separating reality from fantasy. Rather than condemn any particular system of martial art, Bruce absorbed what was useful and discarded what was useless, and he taught us what he considered the "reality" of martial art—simplicity, harmony, and integrity.

This is in many ways comparable to the ultimate beauty that resides in the way young children expresses themselves in the most simple, spontaneous, flowing manner. Their sincerity of emotion just comes forth naturally. Bruce preached to us about the cold facts of life: for example, if you want to become a swimmer, you cannot do so on dry land, you must enter the water. He shared with me and all who studied with him the absolutes: honesty, respect to all, humility, confidence, and the cultivating of an insatiable desire to reach your goal!

When Bruce was alive, he always pushed me in a direction that I believe he would wish all of us to follow: To fulfill to the utmost your physical capabilities which enable you to identify who you really are with humility and pride. Once this is accomplished, the door will open and you will enter the kingdom of philosophical spirituality.

The Seattle curriculum that Bruce entrusted me to teach, and which John has included in the appendix of this book, began with this unique and simple concept of truth and reality.

Even now, my blood becomes feverish when I reflect upon those bygone days when Bruce and I were together. He ingeniously helped me to recapture the days I lost having been interned for five years in an American concentration camp for simply having been born of Japanese descent. I had just graduated from high school and Bruce provided me with a therapy of sorts—just being able to "hang out" and do some of the light-hearted, crazy things that I had missed out on and been deprived of during my internment. The bitterness, negativeness, and the feeling of complete inferiority that plagued me in the days before Bruce Lee came into my life, are—as a direct result of his teachings and my own willingness to apply them—now just water that has passed under the bridge. I realize now that there was a concealed, hidden enrichment that I gleaned from my experiences, both positive and negative, that has served to make me a better person today.

Bruce used to say "He who knows but knows not he knows, he is asleep—awaken him." Although I would not come to appreciate this statement until many years later, I am thankful that he "filled my cup" without my even realizing it, somehow knowing that I "knew not that I knew."

I have many cherished memories of Bruce. We trained together, ate together, went to movies together, and talked about every topic under the sun. I vividly remember appearing with Bruce when he gave martial art demonstrations in Seattle and California, where I experienced the hair-raising effect of facing his punches and kicks, which would explode toward me with the power and speed of a hurricane, only to stop a fraction of an inch from my face. The force of the breeze caused by his blows would literally "part" my hair!

Bruce was my mentor, my sifu, my advisor, and, most importantly, my friend. He embodied the highest principles of the true martial artist.

INTRODUCTION

This book was not written with any intention of presenting a complete textbook on Chinese boxing. To produce such a volume would require too much of the remaining lifetime of its authors. It would be so voluminous that the cost of publication would be prohibitive and would leave our publishers without profit. Finally, about 95 percent of it would be incomprehensible to, and impractical for, about 99 percent of its possible readers.

This book was written for self-defense as taught in China and as used in real emergencies. We have selected only those movements which can be accomplished with but a small expenditure of strength and without previous training or experience.

Finally, let us impress upon you strongly that these movements cannot be mastered without practice, more practice, and still more practice, any more than you can become proficient in tennis, golf, boxing, or any other sport without constant study and practice.

Chinese boxing has been practiced in China for over four thousand years. It consists of ways of fighting without weapons, or against weapons, using the legs, arms, and other parts of the body. Each clan had its own method, differing in some respects from those of each of the others. There were almost as many methods as there were clans.

I wish to express my gratitude to my teacher for many years, Mr. Yip Man, leader of the Wing Chun Chinese Boxing Association (W.C.C.B.A.).

—Bruce Lee

Part 1

WHAT IS GUNG FU?

AN INTRODUCTION
TO CHINESE GUNG FU

The center of the Far Eastern martial arts has been the Chinese art of gung fu, whose principles and techniques pervaded and influenced the different oriental arts of self-defense.

Gung fu, the ancestor of karate, ju-jutsu, etc., is one of the oldest known forms of self-defense and can well be called the concentrated essence of wisdom and profound thoughts on the art of combat. With a four-thousand-year-old background, gung fu has never been surpassed in comprehensiveness and depth of understanding.

Three stages of development

There were three main stages of development in the Chinese art of gung fu. In the midst of antiquity, gung fu was simply a natural, primitive, no-holds-barred type of fighting with hands and feet. Although it was not so scientific, the method nevertheless was natural and free, without any inhibition. The action was not restrained, arrested, or checked. As time went on, the rudimentary techniques of the art were "intellectually" improved further and, although the techniques were definitely superior to the primitive method, the refined scientific art was finite and not as free and natural. Furthermore, by this too philosophical and too scientific, objective approach, the hidden recesses of the mind could not be penetrated. During that stage, most of the techniques consisted of fancy mechanical motion and unnecessary steps toward the desired end. In short, it was a complicated mess.

As the centuries went by, countless generations of the art's practitioners emerged, gradually perfecting it, smoothing out the rough spots, polishing the techniques until gung fu changed into a smooth, flowing "simplified" Way of self-defense. This simplicity was the result of endless exhaustive experiments and profound thought on the original highly complicated method of combat. All techniques became the "one" without opposites, infinite and unceasing, and all movements were stripped to their essential purpose, without any wasted and unnecessary motions. This transformation was influenced greatly by the ideals of Taoism, Ch'an (Zen) and the *I'Ching* at that time.

To illustrate this stage of simplicity, I would like to turn to the Chinese language. About half a century ago, most language experts called the Chinese language "baby talk." They apparently didn't appreciate the word simplicity because they were shocked to find out that the Chinese language has no genders, no cases, no tenses, no voices, no numbers, etc. (Actually what the Chinese language does not have is rather unbelievable!). However, after years of research, the language experts finally found out that this "grammerless" language did have a complicated grammar system like theirs but was later on simplified into the present-day streamlined, smooth-flowing language. Instead of a "baby talk" language, Chinese is the most natural grown-up language in the world.

In school the Chinese children do not have to face the headache of grammar and what they learn is to put the right character into the right order of a sentence—and that's all.

Observe some basic simplification. Instead of saying "two men," the Chinese would say "two man" because here the number "two" already signifies how many. In correct English one says "yesterday I went," but in Chinese, they say "Yesterday I go" for the word "yesterday" has already suggested an event that has occurred in the past. If the Chinese wanted to say "I did that," they said "I finish do that"; for "a man of inability" they say "a no ability man," etc. (These are but a few examples and if the readers are interested they can find out more information from books on that subject.)

The English language, interestingly enough, is doing just the same as the Chinese—moving to simplify its structure and construction. Among the Western languages, English is the most flexible, simple, and practical (note, for instance, the grammar of French and Latin). It is now approaching the stage that the Chinese achieved several thousand years ago. (*Note:* for similar thoughts on the simplicity of movement, please refer to the third section of this book regarding Taoism.)

Returning to the topic of gung fu, the word *gung fu* means "training" or "work" but in the sense of martial art, gung fu means training and discipline toward the *Way* to the object—be it the Way to health promotion, to spiritual cultivation, or to the Way of self-defense.

Geographically, Chinese gung fu was, and indeed, still is, divided into northern and southern schools. The northern schools are generally noted for their kicking (usually high or flying kicks) and their long-range style. The southern schools, on the other hand, are renowned for their hand-to-hand close-range style. Of course, this is not a set rule.

Gung fu is the all-embracing name for all schools of Chinese martial art, such as the Hung system, the White Crane system, the tai-chi ch'uan system, the Wing Chun system, the Praying Mantis system, etc. One can say he knows the Hung or the Lee, but not

gung fu, as the word includes all techniques of all schools, the 72 joint locks, the 36 throws, and the ways of the 18 different weapons. There is no human being alive that knows and can use gung fu as a whole, and even if one could be indiscriminately accepted by all the different schools for instruction, it would take more than one's lifetime to acquire proficiency in all of these varied disciplines.

Gung fu, the prevalent term used in the United States today, is known as *mo suirt* (*wu-shu* in Mandarin) or *gok suirt* (*kuo shu* in Red China, Formosa, and Hong Kong). However, neither of these two terms signifies too much, as *mo suirt*—meaning martial art—can refer to any specific system of martial art, while *gok suirt*—

meaning National art—can refer to any form of art, including music, dancing, and painting.

Still, the term *gung fu* is not used incorrectly in the United States. In fact, it is the most appropriate term for all the different schools. The original meaning of the word *gung fu* is "accumulation of work or training." However, in the sense of martial art, gung fu means training and discipline toward the ultimate reality of the object, whether the object be health promotion, cultivation of mind, or self-protection.

Three stages of cultivation

There are three stages in the cultivation of gung fu. Namely, the Primitive Stage, the Stage of Art, and the Stage of Artlessness. The Primitive Stage is the stage of ignorance in which a person knows nothing of the art of combat and in a fight he simply blocks and hits "instinctively." The second stage (the Stage of Art) begins when he starts his training in gung fu. In his lessons, he is taught the different ways of blocking and striking, the forms, the way to stand, to kick, etc. Unquestionably he has gained a scientific knowledge of combat, but his original "self" and sense of freedom are lost. His mind "stops" at various movements for intellectual analysis and calculations. His action no longer flows by itself. The third stage (the Stage of Artlessness) arrives when his training reaches maturity; his techniques are performed on an almost unconscious level without any interference from his mind. Instead of "I hit," it becomes "it hits!" This is the stage of *cultivated ignorance.* In other words, before I learned martial art, a punch was just like a punch, a kick just like a kick. After I learned martial art, a punch was no longer a punch, a kick no longer a kick. Finally, after I understood martial art, a punch is just like a punch, a kick just like a kick.

These three stages also apply to the various methods being practiced in gung fu. Some methods are rather primitive with jerky, basic blocking and striking; on the whole, they lack the flow and change of combination. Some "sophisticated" systems, on the other

hand, tend to run to ornamentation and get carried away with grace and showmanship. They, whether from the so-called external (firm) or internal (gentle) school, often involve big or fancy motions with a lot of complicated steps or circles toward a single goal. They are too philosophically involved (intellectually bound) and do not want to come off with sophistication. It is like an artist who, not satisfied with drawing a simple snake, proceeds to put four beautiful and shapely feet on the snake! When grasped by the collar, for example, these practitioners would "first unbalance and/or side step" (this, of course, is the divine principle of the circle—in order to do something you must first give) or break loose forcibly by striking the opponent's hand (thus tearing one's shirt), or "flow" with the movement and dissolve by turning or running circles (providing, of course, that your opponent just stands there holding on and watching all of this)—*then* they would strike and/or kick and/or lock and break the joints and/or throw their opponent. However, the direct way is to let him have the pleasure of grasping the collar and simply punch him in the nose! (To some martial artists of distinguishing taste, this would be a little bit unsophisticated, too ordinary and unartful.) On the whole, the followers of these methods are either too intellectually bound or too physically bound and do not wish to see the plain truth.

Which leads us to the schools of profound simplicity, a natural result of exhaustive experimentation of highly sophisticated complexity. All techniques are stripped to their essential purpose and the utmost is now expressed and performed with the minimum of movements and energy. There is no ornamentation or waste, and everything becomes the straightest, most logical simplicity of common-sense (this Stage of Simplicity is not basic or primitive and cannot be achieved without going through the second stage).

As mentioned earlier, the object of gung fu is for health promotion, cultivation of mind, and self-protection. Toward this end, its philosophy is based on the integral parts of the philosophies of Taoism, Ch'an (Zen), and I'Ching—the ideals of attuning with nature, and of harmony of yin and yang are stressed (please see the next section on yin and yang). The whole idea is not to dominate your opponent but to achieve harmony with him. Just as a butcher preserves his knife by cutting along the line of the bone, a gung fu man preserves himself by complementing—and not opposing—the force of his opponent. In order to reconcile oneself to the changing movements of the opponent, a gung fu man should first of all understand the true meaning of yin/yang—the basic structure of gung fu.

ON YIN AND YANG

The basic structure of gung fu is based on the theory of yin and yang, a pair of mutually complementary and interdependent forces that act continuously, without cessation, in this universe. To the Chinese, harmony is regarded as the basic principle of the world order, as a cosmic field of force in which the yin and the yang are eternally complementary and eternally changing. European dualism sees physical and metaphysical as two separate entities, at best as cause and effect, but never paired like sound and echo, or light and shadow, as in the Chinese symbol of all happening: the yin/yang.

The above figure shows the symbol of tai chi or, in Cantonese, the *tai kik* in which the yin and yang are two interlocking parts of one whole, each containing within its confines the qualities of its complementaries. Etymologically the characters of yin and yang mean darkness and light. The ancient character of yin, the black part of the circle, is a drawing of clouds and hill.

Yin can represent anything in the universe as:

- negativeness • passiveness • gentleness • internal
- insubstantiality • femaleness • moon • darkness • night, etc.

The other complementary part of the circle is yang. The lower part of the character signifies slanting sunrays, while the upper part represents the sun. Yang can represent anything as:

- positiveness • activeness • firmness • external
- substantiality • maleness • sun • brightness • day, etc.

The common mistake of the Western world is to identify these two forces, yin and yang, as dualistic; that is, yang being the opposite of yin, and vice versa. As long as this "oneness" is viewed as two separate entities, realization of the Tao of gung fu won't be achieved. In reality things are "whole" and cannot be separated into parts. When I say the heat makes me perspire, the heat and perspiring are just one process as they are coexistent and the one could not exist but for the other. Just as an object needs a subject, the person in question is not taking an independent position but is acting as an assistant.

The dualistic philosophy, however, reigned supreme in Europe, dominating the development of Western science. But with the advent of atomic physics, findings based on demonstrable experiment were seen to negate the dualistic theory and the trend of thought since then has led back toward the *monistic conception* of the ancient Taoists. In atomic physics no distinction is recognized between matter and energy; nor is it possible to make such a distinction, since they are in reality one essence, or at least two poles of the same unit. It is no longer possible, as it was in the mechanistic scientific era, to absolutely define weight, length, or time, etc., as the work of Einstein, Plank, Whitehead, and Jeans has demonstrated it is.

In the same way, the Taoist philosophy, against the background of which acupuncture had its origin and developed, is essentially monistic. The Chinese conceived the entire universe as activated by two principles, the yang and the yin, the positive and negative, and they considered that nothing that exists, either animate or so-called inanimate, does so, except by virtue of the ceaseless interplay of these two forces. Matter and energy, yang and yin, heaven and earth, are conceived of as essentially one or as two coexistent poles of one indivisible whole. Again, it is not possible to make a distinction between matter and energy because they are in reality two poles of the same unit. Things do have their complementaries, and complementaries coexist and, instead of being mutually exclusive, are in fact mutually dependent and are a function each of the other.

Natural balance inherent in all things

In the yin/yang symbol there is a white spot on the black part and a black spot on the white part. This is to illustrate the balance in life, for nothing can survive long by going to either extremes, be it pure yin (negativeness) or pure yang (positiveness). Extreme heat kills as does extreme cold. No violent extremes endure. Nothing lasts but sober moderation. Notice that the stiffest tree is most easily cracked, while the bamboo or willow survive by bending with the wind. Firmness without pliancy is like a barrel without water, and pliancy without firmness is like water without a barrel. In gung fu, yang (positiveness) should be concealed in yin (negativeness, which is represented symbolically by the white spot on the black part), and yin (negativeness) in yang (positiveness, which is represented symbolically by the black spot on the white part). A gung fu man, then, should be soft—yet not yielding; firm—yet not hard.

When the movement of yin/yang flows into extremes, reaction sets in. For when yang goes to the extreme, it changes back to yin and vice versa, each being the cause and result of the other. For example, when one works to the extreme, he becomes tired and has to rest (a transition from yang to yin). After resting, he can work again (a transition of yin back to yang). This incessant changing of yin/yang is always continuous.

Therefore, in gung fu one should be in harmony with, and not in opposition against, the force of one's opponent. Suppose A applies force on B; B shouldn't oppose or completely give way to it (for these are but the two extreme opposites of B's reaction to A's force). Instead, B should complete A's force with a lesser force (firmness in gentleness) and lead him to the direction of his own movement. This spontaneous assisting of A's movement as he aims it will result in his own defeat. Again, as the butcher preserves his knife by cutting along the barrier of the bone and not against it, a gung fu man preserves himself by following the movement of his opponent without opposition.

ON BRIDGING THE GAP OF YIN AND YANG

Gentleness and firmness (yin and yang) are two "interdependent" and "complementary" forces in the Chinese art of gung fu, and the aim is the attainment and maintenance of perfect balance between these two forces.

Gentleness/firmness is one inseparable force of once unceasing interplay of movement. If a person riding a bicycle wishes to go somewhere, for example, he can't pump on both the pedals at the same time or not pump on them at all. In order to move forward he pumps on one pedal while simultaneously releasing the other. So the movement of going forward requires this "oneness" of pumping and releasing. Pumping then is the result of releasing and vice versa, each being the cause of the other.

This oneness of things is a characteristic of the Chinese mind. In the Chinese language events are looked on as a whole because their meaning is derived from each other. For instance, the characters for good and bad are different. However, when combined, the word *quality* is formed. So in order to form the whole word *quality*, half of the positive of and half of the negative of is necessary. The characters for long and for short together (long/short) mean the "length" of something. The character for buying and that for selling, when written together, form the new word *trade*.

The same thing applies to the movements in gung fu, which is always the ceaseless interplay of the two forces of gentleness and firmness. They are conceived of as essentially one, or as two coexistent forces of one indivisible whole. Their meaning (gentleness/firmness) is derived *from* each other and their completion *through* each other.

Many times I have heard instructors from different schools claim that their systems of gentleness (yin) require absolutely no strength (strength has become an ugly word to them), and that with merely a flick of one's little finger, one can send his three-hundred-pound helpless opponent flying through the air. We must face the fact that strength, though used in a much more refined way, is necessary in combat, and that an average opponent doesn't charge in blindly with his head down (not even a football tackler will do this!). He, too, might possess speed and snap and some rudimentary knowledge of fighting.

Some instructors, on the other hand, claim that with their "super powerful system" one can smash through any defense. Once again we must realize that a person does move and change just as a bamboo that moves back and forth in a storm to "dissolve" the strong wind. So neither gentleness (yin) nor firmness (yang) holds any more than one half of a broken whole which, fitted together, forms the true Way of gung fu. Remember that in order to go somewhere, one can't pump on both the bicycle pedals at the same time or not pump on them at all.

Gentleness alone can't forever dissolve away great force, nor can sheer brute force forever subdue one's foe. In order to survive in combat, the harmonious interfusion of gentleness and firmness as a whole is necessary, sometimes one dominating and sometimes the other, in a wave-like succession. The movement will then truly flow; for the true fluidity of movement is in its changeability.

Instead of opposing force by force, a gung fu man completes his opponent's movement by accepting his flow of energy as he aims it, and defeats him by borrowing his own force. This, in gung fu, is known as The Law of Adaptation. In order to reconcile one-self to the changing movements of the opponent, a gung fu man should first of all understand the true meaning of gentleness and firmness.

There is no dislocation in the Way of gung fu movement. They are done with flowing continuity like the movement of a river that is forever flowing without a moment of cessation or standing still. As soon as a movement is approximately finished, it immediately flows into another one without stopping. Thus, defense and attack are alternately producing one another.

Firmness and gentleness in the Chinese art of gung fu are not isolated, but coalescent, and the same goes for the various movements such as attack and defense, expansion and contraction, pushing and pulling, etc.

I've learned a lot from observing nature (see "A Moment of Understanding" in Part 3 of this book). Such theories of movement and utilization of energy are brought about from the regularity of the tides and from the effect of the wind upon branches or grass. I've established my own postulate on the utilization of energy and the Way of movements of gung fu. The movement of gung fu is like that of a string of pearls. The pearls are the techniques used and the string is the linking of each technique. The utilization of energy and movement in gung fu should flow on continuously without cessation. There is no broken or interrupted action. As soon as a technique is finished, it begins to melt and blend into another one. Expansion is interdependent with contraction and vice versa.

The common mistake most people make is the punching of one hand while pulling the other all the way back. I've given this mistake a description of the "beads without the string." Observe the following illustrations:

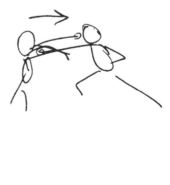

The Tao of Gung Fu

The "beads" in this example are the individual techniques, and without the string to link them, they are going to fall apart. In order to achieve the oneness of these movements of negative and positive, the gap between punching and pulling should be bridged. When punching, a little pulling (by itself) is immediately followed, and when pulling, a little pressing forward is concealed. The mistakes committed in the previous sketches are based on pure advancing yang (sheer punching) and pure withdrawing yin (sheer pulling).

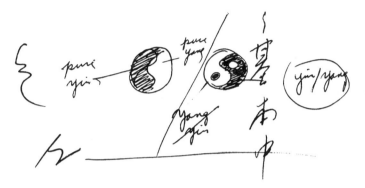

Any practitioner of martial art should therefore consider both the softness and firmness as equals in importance and unavoidably interdependent of one another. The rejection of either gentleness or firmness will lead to separation and separation runs to extreme. Understand the fact that firmness and gentleness are not isolated, but coalescent; they are complementary as well as contrastive and in their interfusion make up the oneness. The idea of opposition results when we single out firmness and treat it as distinct from gentleness. Tall, for example, once distinguished, suggests its opposite: short. However, in order to distinguish tallness, shortness is necessary for the comparison and tallness cannot exist without shortness. Firmness actually is gentleness, and gentleness is firmness, each is the cause and result of the other (they are alternately producing one another). One shouldn't therefore favor too much on either gentleness or firmness alone so that he can truly appreciate the "good/bad" of them. Remember, gentleness *versus* firmness is not the situation, but gentleness/firmness as a *oneness* is the Tao.

Part 2

SOME TECHNIQUES OF GUNG FU

THE FUNDAMENTALS OF GUNG FU

The ready stance

The requirements of the various parts of the body in assuming the *by-jong* or "ready stance" are as follows:

1. The Head: Hold your head as you would naturally, that is, it should be straight without inclination to either side. You should have a feeling that the head is pushing upward. Your neck muscles should be relaxed without tensing. Your facial expression must be natural without any sign of emotion (in other words, simply a standard expression). Your tongue must be pressed against the palate and your mouth naturally closed. The point of your chin should be slightly tucked in. If you use your imagination, you can accomplish all of the above effortlessly and naturally. Remember—just be natural!

2. The Trunk (chest and back): According to the old doctrines of the internal clan of gung fu, the chest must be sucked in and the back slightly raised. This allows your breathing to go down to the abdomen; nevertheless the posture does not suggest that you should be a hunchback. Remember that all this must be done naturally. The chest muscles must be completely relaxed and not tensed so that the breathing will be regulated.

3. The Waist: The waist is the mainspring of the movements of the body. The movements of the limbs are slow and short, while those of the waist are free and long (waist—big axis, limbs—small axis). Remember therefore that one turning of a big axis is equivalent to hundreds of turnings of a small axis. The waist plays an important part in walking, running, standing, or sitting. In gung fu the waist is one of the most important parts in connecting the movements of the upper and lower body. During practice, whether in advancing or retreating, the waist is consciously lowered downward; never tense it up by arching forward or backward so that it hinders the natural movements. All these must be done naturally.

4. The Hip: The hip must never stick out during lowering of the body.

5. The Legs: The legs are very important in gung fu, as they involve the whole balance of the body. Your step should be firm, yet light and capable of changing. The knee and the thigh must be relaxed, with the knee slightly bent. Separate clearly the yin and yang among the steps. Your body weight should be distributed with 70 percent of the weight resting on the rear foot and 30 percent resting on the lead foot. This weight distribution will allow you full use of the front leg as a counter kicking weapon.

6. The Shoulders and Elbows: The shoulders and elbows should be relaxed and lowered. The fingers of the lead hand should be pointing forward and up toward the opponent's nose, with the lead arm

bent at the elbow at a forty-five–degree angle. The left hand should be held parallel to the right elbow with the fingers pointing up.

The centerline theory

Imagine that your body is divided by a line that runs from between your legs through the top of your head. In gung fu this is called *joan sien*, or the centerline theory. It is the base from which all defense and attack are deployed. You must always have your centerline guarded with one of your hands at all times, and whenever you change the position of your hands, regardless of your position, you must always endeavor to protect the centerline.

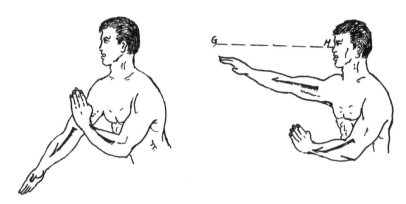

It has been determined that the ideal distance your lead elbow should be from the centerline is three inches. This allows you to employ the immovable-elbow theory (see the following section), which is fundamental for attack and defense in many styles of gung fu.

Additionally, the centerline theory allows you to generate more power in your techniques as it serves to coordinate both arm and body, enabling a gung fu man to employ his entire body weight with each strike. Using arm force alone is indeed a characteristic of the untrained person (in fact, a lot of instructors are practitioners of that), and since striking is mainly used in gung fu, I'll discuss the relationship of arm power and body power (waist or hip movement) in landing a punch. In order to facilitate comprehension of what is involved in combining the waist with the arm, I've divided the human body into two halves with an imaginary centerline as in Figure 1.

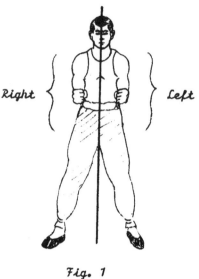

Fig. 1

Figure 2 shows a person releasing his right side and propelling his body weight (as in an ordinary right-hand punch) by bracing himself on his left foot, which acts as the hinge around which his right-side body weight and power rotates. The hip and shoulders are driven first to the imaginary centerline, then the arm comes into play "explosively." The whole idea is to transfer the weight—via your

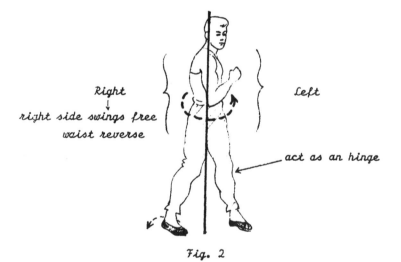

Fig. 2

strike—to the opponent's target area before the weight transfers to the left leg. That is also why in stepping in to strike, the leading foot should not land first, or the body weight will rest upon the floor instead of being behind the striking hand. Of course, all these are coordinated very, very fast, but the waist does come a split second faster.

From this centerline I was able to construct a nucleus and, later on, able to jump away from the nucleus and establish such things as out-of-line and broken rhythm counterattack. Thus, my theory states:

1. Learn the center.
2. Keep the center.
3. Dissolve the center.

Or, it can be stated more generally:

1. Learn the rules.
2. Keep to the rules.
3. Dissolve the rules.

Emphasis must be made to students of gung fu to strike with their entire body behind their technique because, in terms of force and power, the arms have but one quarter of the force of the body when set in motion. Secondly, the movements of the waist are long and free, while those of the arms are short. You can say that one turning of a large axis is equivalent to many turnings of a small axis. Also, the arms can only exert their maximum strength toward the end of the movement—therefore, the arms are the vehicle of force that is released by the body through this centerline idea. Boxing also makes use of this centerline theory but expresses it in too big a motion. It is all right at first, but later on it should be guided by the principle of simplicity—to express the utmost in the minimum of movements and energy.

The immovable-elbow theory

It is important when assuming the by-jong that the elbow of your lead arm remain immovable. With your elbow in a fixed position approximately three inches in front of your body, you'll note that your hand and forearm are free to move in any direction. If you en-vision a rectangle that has been stood on its end, with its bottom boundary being your groin area, its top boundary being your eye-brows, and its remaining two sides being each of your respective shoulders, you will understand the parameters of movement—up and down and sideways—that your arms can travel. Further imagine that there is an invisible perpendicular line that intersects your elbow. If your lead arm is pressed, hold to the core or centerline. Do not give it up, even if it means your entire body must move, and never allow your elbow to dip below your navel.

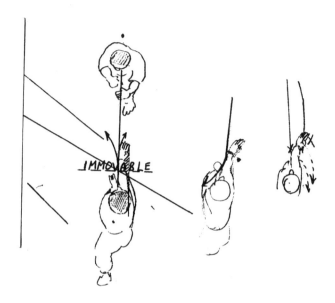

In gung fu, the immovable elbow is called *but doan jiang* and is one of the cornerstones of the Wing Chun system. In theory, it is likened to a hurricane of which the eye is always still, but its periphery is tremendously forceful and constantly moving. In other words, the motionless center of vortices appears in manifestation as motion, which increases in velocity in the manner of a whirlpool or tornado (whose epicenter is still) from nucleus to periphery. The nucleus is in reality, whereas the vortex is a phenomenon in the form of a multidimensional force field.

Concentrate your energy at the immovable instead of dispersing in scattered activities. In other words, hold to the core.

The four gates

The immovable-elbow position is fundamental to all parrying, deflecting, and blocking in gung fu (particularly in the art of Wing

　　　　　　　　　　　　　　　　　　　　The Tao of Gung Fu

Chun). Defense in gung fu takes place along the four boundaries through the application of the four corner parries. The four corner parries take place within the four parameters of the rectangle described in the section on the immovable elbow; the groin area at the bottom, the eyebrow area at the top, and the area just past the shoulders on both sides. The corners are divided into four equal regions, or gates: the top portion of the forward-hand side (the upper outside gate), the top portion of the rear-hand side (the upper inner gate), the lower portion of the forward-hand side (the lower outside gate), and the lower portion of the rear-hand side (the lower inner gate).

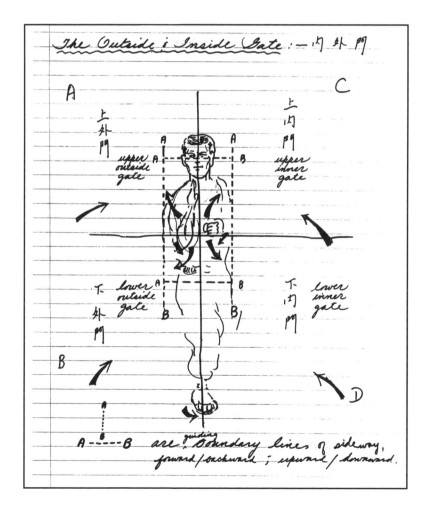

The eight basic blocking positions (from by-jong)

All attacks directed toward either of the outside gates (i.e., lower or upper outside gate) are to be blocked to the outside, while all attacks directed toward either of the inside gates (i.e., lower or upper inside gate) are blocked inwardly. Furthermore, there is a forward and rear portion of each gate, which are to be guarded by the forward and rear hands, respectively. That is, if a punch is not deflected by your lead forearm as it comes toward you, by the time it reaches your chest area, your rear hand should have it taken care of (whether it travels to the upper gates or the lower gates).

Blocking Positions (the right stance)

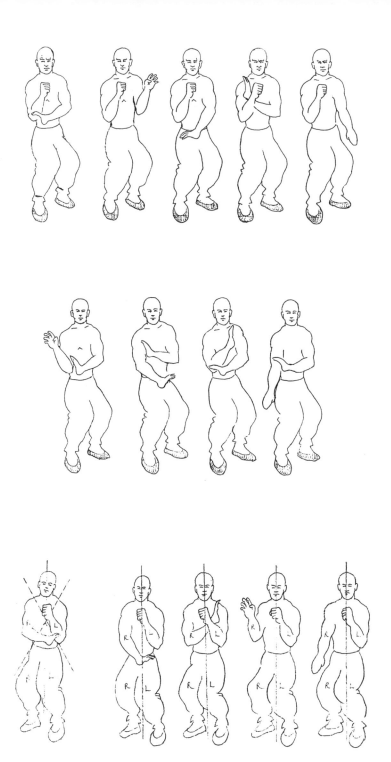

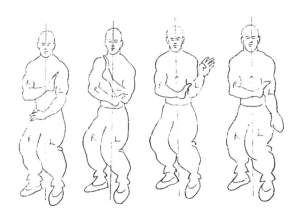

Additional considerations on the fundamentals

The structure of the Wing Chun gung fu school

(The simplicity of the truly sophisticated)

Note: All diagrams are in the ready position (by-jong)

The Seven Stars

In gung fu, your opponent (assuming he is unarmed) has seven "natural" weapons, called "stars" or "parts" of the body, that can be used to strike you. These seven stars are:

1. Hand   2. Leg   3. Elbow   4. Head
5. Shoulder   6. Knee   7. Thigh

Watch out for your opponent's seven stars or parts.

The three fronts

Your opponent's seven stars can only reach you through three channels of attack. These channels of attack are called the "three gates" or the "three fronts," because they are situated directly:

1. In *front* of your eyes
2. In *front* of your hands
3. In *front* of your legs

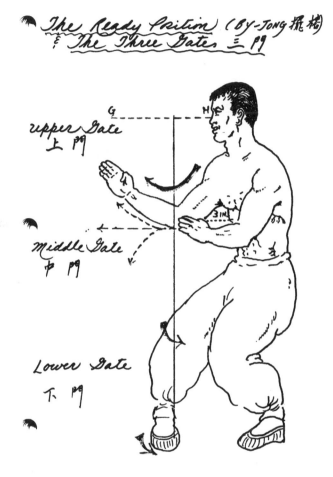

The Ready Position (BY-JONG 飛標)
& The Three Gates 三 門

upper Gate
上 門

middle Gate
中 門

Lower Gate
下 門

Footwork

When in combat, one's stance should be slightly shorter (but not too short, to avoid being pushed off balance) in order to keep the leading leg and foot out of range of a sudden attack. Unless there is a tactical reason for acting otherwise, gaining and breaking of ground is executed by means of small and rapid steps, and all hand movements (as indicated in the section on the centerline theory) are to be combined with waist and footwork.

Practice sliding your lead foot forward in ten-inch steps and then immediately drag your rear foot up an equal distance once your weight has shifted to the lead foot. Conversely, as a further aid to mobility, you should practice shifting your weight back to the rear foot and then repeat the process. Continue on in this manner until you develop proficiency in your mobility. Once this is achieved, you can begin to use this footwork in various directions, always making sure that the placement of your lead foot is determined by the direction your opponent turns.

The Way of facing (footwork)

Since it is crucially important to guard your centerline with the immovable-elbow position, it is imperative to know how to face your opponent (*jiue ying*). When you face your opponent, you are able to preserve your centerline and make it impermeable. If you do not keep facing your opponent (nose-to-nose), you are susceptible to your opponent's attack.

The Tao of Gung Fu

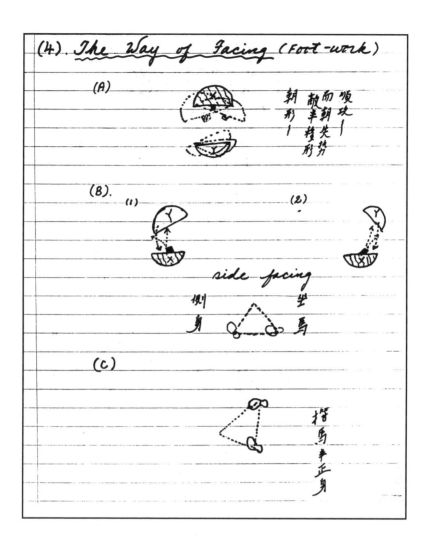

The four rules of successful footwork

In order for your movement to be successful, and to gauge the fighting distance correctly, four rules must be followed:

1. Maintain total sensitivity of the aura.

2. Be totally alive and natural in your motions.

3. Maintain the correct distance between yourself and your opponent.

4. Maintain the correct placement of your body.

Training to enhance footwork

You can increase your ability to control your legs through medium-posture squatting exercises and ape-imitation movements such as low walking. Also helpful in developing balance, mobility, and body feel are exercises such as skipping, running, squatting (both with and without weights), and alternate (i.e., standing) splits. You should also practice stepping to both sides and their variations while employing your kicking tools and hand tools, all the while covering your centerline and hand and knee positions. For example, when side-stepping to the left, your right or lead leg should cross over in front of your rear leg, in order to protect your groin area. This is immediately followed by a lateral step of equal distance by the rear or left leg so that the by-jong is once more assumed. Conversely, when side-stepping to the right, your left or rear leg should cross behind your lead leg to be followed immediately by the lead leg, thereby allowing you to reassume the by-jong position.

THE BASIC STRIKING POINTS OF GUNG FU

There is only one basic principle of self-defense: You must apply the most effective weapon as soon as possible to the most vulnerable point of your enemy. In this chapter you'll find diagrams showing the most effective weapons given to you by nature and the most vulnerable points of the body. Please note that all of these movements are serious and dangerous and should be used only when actually necessary for self-defense.

Weapons

   a. Used against the solar plexus.

   b. Used against the junction of the nose and forehead, or between the upper lip and the inside of the neck.

   c. Used against the body.

   d. Used against the eyes.

   e. Used against the solar plexus or the jaw.

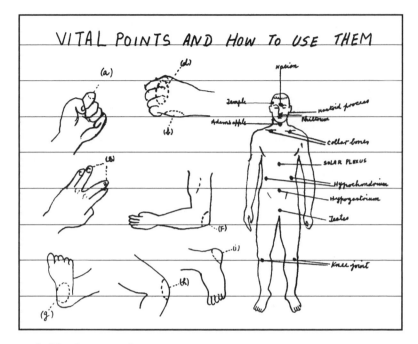

VITAL POINTS AND HOW TO USE THEM

f. Used against the testes.

g. Used against the crotch, abdomen, or testes.

h. Used from prone position against the knee, crotch, abdomen, jaw, or chin.

Another view of weapons and their applications

The first hand weapon to learn to use effectively should be the straight punch with a vertical fist, then the finger jab, then the peacock eye (one-knuckle fist), and the chop choy (four-knuckle fist). *Note:* The chop choy and peacock eye are only effective when applied against boney areas or targets like eyes, throat, and temple areas.

There are various kinds of strikes—it depends on where you hit and what weapon you will be using. To the eyes you would use fingers. And then there is the bent-arm strike, using the waist to turn it into a back fist which can be deployed either high (to the head) or low (to the groin). Kicks are employed to areas such as the groin, knee, shin, or instep. Although I said at the outset that there is only one basic principle of self-defense, it is better to break it into

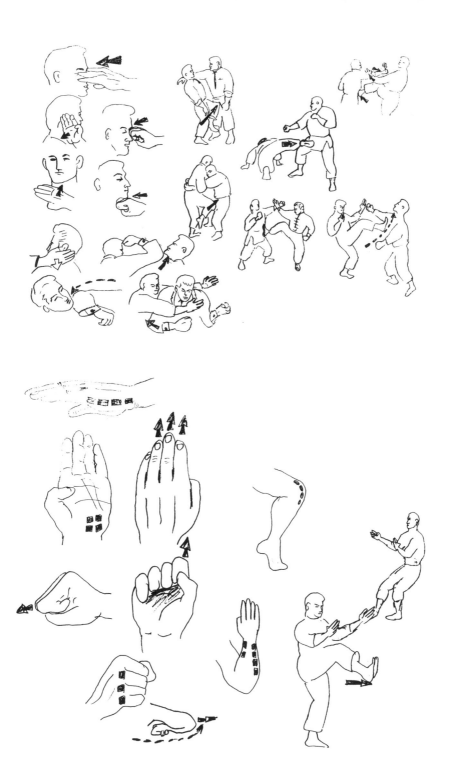

Some Techniques of Gung Fu

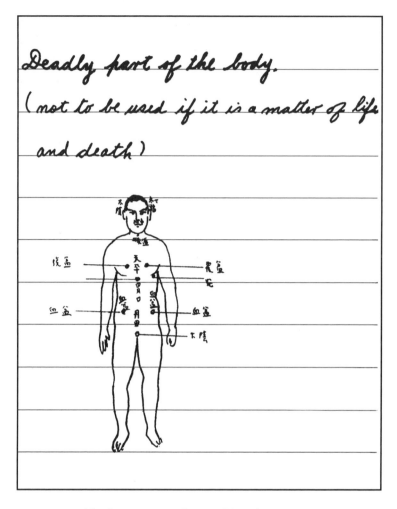

sections and look at it more thoroughly. These sections are:

1. The most effective weapon
2. Speed
3. The point to attack or counterattack

The most effective weapon

Given a choice of the most effective weapon, I would always choose the leg. It is longer than the arm and can deal a heavier blow, and it is much more powerful. So, should anyone approach you, your kick would make contact before his punch, if both commence at the same speed.

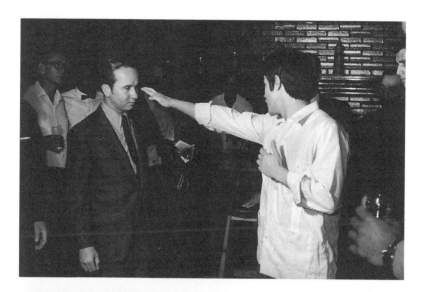

Speed

In all but the rarest of situations there exists no time to consider the type of defense or weapon to use. Obviously, if your kick does not commence, his punch will land first, and your defense is useless. Only training can produce results (I can help you with this). If you do not consider a few minutes of training worthwhile, and think the

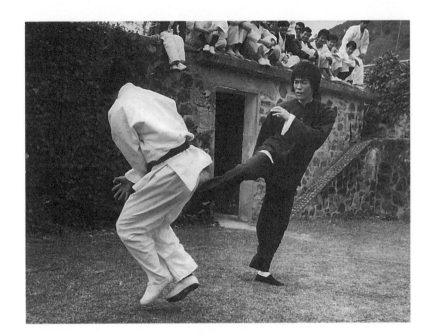

chance of assault is small, you are one of those people who encourages thugs to attack, and no one can help you should an emergency arise.

The point to attack or counterattack

Among the most vulnerable points for your counter if attacked by a man are the groin, eyes, abdomen, and knee.

INTRODUCING THE WING CHUN STRAIGHT PUNCH

The art of straight hitting (punching in a straight and direct line) is the foundation of scientific skill. It is the end result of thousands of years of careful analysis and thought. The straight punch requires tremendous speed and intelligence to use. It was observed that a straight punch has less distance to travel en route to its target than do round or circular arm blows (all of the above also apply to kicking as well), which means that it will always reach the mark before these other strikes. In addition, the straight punch using a vertical fist (ch'ung chuie) is more accurate than hooks and swings and makes full use of the arm's potential reach.

It is important *not* to initiate the straight punch from the hip, the way of delivery of most other schools of martial art. This way of delivery is unrealistic and exposes your torso too much upon delivery, in addition to adding too much unnecessary distance for the punch to travel toward your opponent. Instead of initiating from the shoulder, the punch is thrown from the center of the body, in the form of a vertical fist (i.e., thumb facing up), and travels on an upward arc that peaks straight in front of your own nose. The nose here is the extension of the centerline of your torso. You can generate extra impact power by keeping your wrist turned slightly downward during delivery and then straightening it immediately upon impact to add torque or a corkscrew effect to its impact.

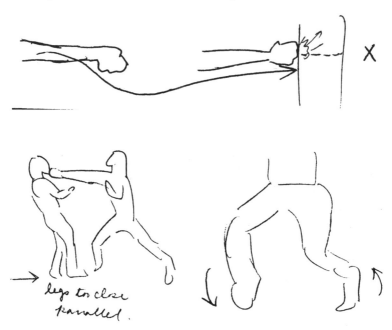

legs too close parallel.

Your punch should be aimed at the center of your opponent's face. The striking area of the punch should be the last or bottom three knuckles of the fist, and you should be dropping your body weight behind each punch.

The punch should be able to be delivered at a moment's notice and at any range (again, do not start it from the waist) and should end with a snap. It should start off with speed but with no energy or force, and concentrate all of your energy at the point of impact.

Do not use only arm power in striking, but strike with correct timing, footwork, plus waist motion and mental aiming. This mental aiming is to aim two inches further or any part of the body to be

The Tao of Gung Fu

struck. When stepping forward to hit, do not let your foot land first so that everything will be behind the striking hand.

Do not drop the other hand when striking; for example, when the right hand hits high, the left should be below the right elbow for protection. In the same way when the left hand hits low, the right hand should be in front of the chest.

Relaxation and follow-through

Relaxation is essential for faster and more powerful punching. Let your straight punch shoot out loosely and easily, do not tighten up or clench the fist of your punching hand until the moment of impact. All punches should end with a snap "several inches behind the target." Thus you punch *through* the opponent instead of *at* him.

The advantages of the lead punch (a summary)

1. Faster—the shortest distance between two points is a straight line.
2. More accurate—"chooses the straightest course." Thus less chance of missing and is surer than other punches.
3. Balance is less distributed—safer.
4. Less injurious to one's hand.
5. Greater frequency of hits—more damage can be done.
6. Reduces the chances of missing because opponent has less time for blocking.

Regular straight punch versus gung fu straight punch

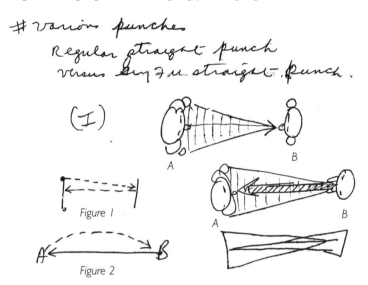

various punches
Regular straight punch
versus gung fu straight punch.

(工)

B

Figure 1

A

B

A

Figure 2

The straight punch is the fastest, most accurate punch in gung fu. Note how it proceeds from B to A in a straight line, with no wasted motion, unlike A's curve line punch to B.

Some additional gung fu hand strikes

[basic — not include
other system]

穿掌 摆指
finger jab

The Tao of Gung Fu

掌法.

① 陰.

Finger jab (straight)

② 挑掌

Finger jab (upward slant)

③ 劈掌

edge of the hand.

Edge-of-hand strike

④ 蓋掌
back palm

Back-palm strike

⑤ 正搨
fan palm

Fan-palm strike

⑥ 反搨
back reverse fan palm

Back fan-palm strike

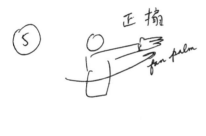

⑦ 印掌 heel penetrating palm

Heel (penetrating) palm strike

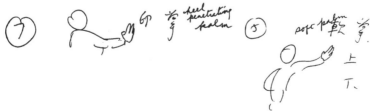

⑧ soft palm 軟掌
上
下.

Open-hand or soft-palm strike

Facing opponent B in ready (by-jong) position.

A slaps B's hand out of the centerline to open a direct path to B's throat

Still trapping B's lead hand with his left hand, A strikes B's throat with a back fan-palm strike.

A backfist could also be employed instead of a back fan-palm strike, resulting in equal success.

The Tao of Gung Fu

The straight blast

The straight punch, when thrown in alternating fashion for several series, is called the straight blast. I consider this form of multiple straight punching the heart of successful close-range attack. Just like the straight punch, all punches should be thrown in long, oval patterns and grouped together in quick succession. This will force your opponent into a defensive posture, thus taking him out of attack mode and also expose his centerline in addition to providing a form of offensive blocking/parrying against in-coming punches. In short, the straight blast is a valuable technique to learn because it is easy to develop, easy to combine with other techniques (such as a finger jab, back fist, or shin kick), and very hard to defend against as most people are inexperienced in defending their centerline area.

BLOCKING/STRIKING TECHNIQUES

I have said before that instead of opposing force with force, a gung fu man completes his opponent's movement by accepting his flow of energy as he aims it, and defeats him by borrowing his own force. In order to reconcile oneself to the changing movements of the opponent, a gung fu man should first of all understand the true meaning of the yin and the yang—the basic structure of gung fu.

Those who view blocking and striking as two separate entities do not fully comprehend the reality of yin/yang. This is the fault of pure striking (yang) and pure withdrawing (yin), which can be illustrated in the following symbol:

It is like a string of beads without the string to link them together. In order to bridge the gap between striking and blocking, the interfusion of the two as a whole is necessary. Thus, the above symbol should be changed to the symbol of yin/yang:

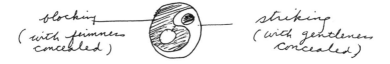

The receptive (yin) is the perfect complementary of firmness (yang); it doesn't combat strength but completes it.

Be soft, yet not yielding; firm, yet not hard.

Remember that firmness is brought to life by gentleness and gentleness is activated and led by firmness.

To be bent is to be straight.

The Tao of Gung Fu

True gentleness is like a pliable reed in the wind; it neither opposes nor gives way. The gentleness accommodates itself to the strength of the firmness to make it its own. There is neither purpose nor effort in receptiveness; the opponent's techniques are your techniques.

Gentleness opens when it moves and closes when at rest.

Yielding overcomes anything stronger than itself; its strength is boundless. Therefore, follow till the moment when the opposing force reaches its limit and begins to decline.

What is adaptation? It is like the immediacy of the shadow adjusting itself to the moving body. What is the highest state of yielding? It is like clutching water. What is gentleness? It is like a spring; if one presses it down, it only springs up higher. What is true stillness? Stillness in movement. What is the purpose of firmness and gentleness? The purpose of firmness is to keep one from getting too lax, while the purpose of gentleness is to keep one from getting too hard. Nothing can survive long by going to extremes.

There is no dislocation in the Way of gung fu movement. The techniques are done with flowing continuity like the movement of a river that is forever flowing without a moment of cessation or standing still. As soon as one movement is completed, it immediately flows into another one without stopping. Thus defense and attack are alternately producing one another.

"To defend is to attack, and to attack is to defend" is, indeed, becoming a cheap statement uttered by all self-defense instructors. Here let us look into the real meaning of this statement by some illustrations of simultaneous attack/defense.

You'll note that during striking, blocking is concealed and during blocking, striking is concealed (yin/yang).

Position—Opponents stand facing each other.

Action—Opponent attempts a blow to the face with his right hand. As the blow comes, quickly use your left hand and push opponent's hand aside. At the same time, your right fist must come out at once and hit your opponent's face.

Position—Opponents stand facing each other.

Action—Opponent intends to hit you on the hypochondrium with his right hand. Quickly use your left hand to stop his blow coming. At the same time, hit him in the solar plexus. Usually, when he gets it, he will turn to the left and try to hit you with his left hand. Hit him again, as we have described.

Position—Opponents stand facing each other.

Action—Opponent hits you on your face with his right hand. You then quickly move your right hand and grasp his right arm. At the same time, use your left fist and hit him on the temple.

Position—Opponents stand facing each other.

Action—Opponent attempts to attack you in the face with his right fist. Quickly move your left hand upward and stop the blow. Then hit straight on his chest with your palm.

Note: All these actions must be done as rapidly as possible.

Position—Opponents stand facing each other.

Action—You intend to attack your opponent's face with your left hand, but he is too clever for you. He defends himself by bringing his right hand upward and stops your blow from coming. When his hand touches you, however, you must quickly go downward and hit him on the rib or belly.

Some Techniques of Gung Fu

Figure 1. A and B facing each other in ready position.

Figure 2. In one motion, A locks B's right hand and strikes his throat simultaneously (note the locking of B's leg for prevention of kicks).

Figure 3. B blocks A's right by slapping it away.

Figure 4. Flowing with B's slapping hand without resisting, A traps B's left hand and counters with a backfist.

Figures 5 and 6. Closing in, A comes in with two straight punches as shown in these two pictures. (Observe how B is "locked" without any striking of kicking room.)

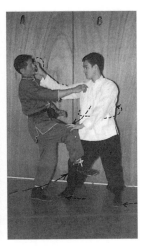

Figure 7. A straight punches to B's face.

Figure 8. Advancing, B deflects A's punch and strikes him simultaneously by turning his waist. The deflection should be outward and upward without over-reaching and, thus going off the body.

Figure 9. A attempts a right straight kick. Closing the distance, B blocks the kick and claws A's eye simultaneously with the striking (right) hand. All of the above movements move in one unit the moment B feels the jerking and relaxation of A's right shoulder and arm.

CLOSE-RANGE GUNG FU— THE STICKING HANDS METHOD OF WING CHUN

Chi sao, the so-called art of sticking hands, is a unique method of training from the Wing Chun style, a southern Chinese style, headed by Mr. Yip Man of Hong Kong. It was actually from Mr. Yip that I took up the style of Wing Chun. Let me preface what I'm about to share with you on this unique method of cultivating sensitivity in one's arms by stating that it is next to impossible to learn proper chi sao from a book.

To learn chi sao properly requires an expert instructor who guides his student step by step and feeds him the right flow. In the hands of a novice, chi sao can turn into a jerky wrestling match. Such strenuous practice will not only hinder understanding, but will lead to instant countering by a sharp opponent.

Chi sao is a flowing energy exercise in which we attach our hands to the opponent's hands and forget ourselves by following the movements of his hands, leaving our mind free to make its own counter-movement without deliberation. When the opponent expands, we contract; when he contracts, we expand—to fit our movements harmoniously into his attack without anticipating or rushing the action, but simply continuing the flow. Flowing energy properly through your hands is like water flowing through a hose. If the water is turned on and off quickly, the hose will jerk. Instead, our defense should follow his attack without a moment's interruption, so that there will be no two separate movements to be known as "attack" and "defense." The important thing is not to attempt to control the attack by resisting it with force (either physical or mental), but rather to control it by going with it, thus not asserting oneself against nature. All these are simply based on the harmonious interchanging of the theory of yin/yang. As long as we plan our actions, we are still using strength and will not be able to feel our opponent's movements, thus failing to comprehend the true application of yin and yang.

In the Wing Chun style, chi sao has both the one-handed and the two-handed practice. By rolling their hands in harmony, as well as in contrast, the practitioners cultivate the flowing energy. The practitioner should keep the flow constant and fill every possible gap in each rolling and turning. As training goes on, the more this energy becomes like water, and the narrower the crack through which its flow can pass.

From the positions in chi sao, each practitioner tries to score squarely on one another. With the flowing energy, the defender "floats" and "dissolves" the opponent's force, like a boat tossing safely among the turbulent waves, so as to borrow the attacker's force to complete his counter. In view of this, the two practitioners are actually two halves of one whole.

Except in the case of one-hand positions, all the others in chi sao are elbows in. This elbow-in position is important in Wing Chun as it acts as a deflecting, auxiliary force should the wrist fail to detect the sudden increase of pressure from the opponent's attack. As mentioned elsewhere in this book, the elbow should be the immovable center, while the forearm and hand are pliable in their

adaptations and changes. So, the hands in chi sao should be soft but not yielding; forceful and firm, but not hard or rigid.

Offensively, Wing Chun's chi sao utilizes mainly straight, forward energy; defensively, it makes use of a deflecting arc as well as straight penetrative lines. The practitioner of the Wing Chun style keeps to the nucleus, letting his opponent move around the circumference. He also learns to move straight from the center out, or "just enough" from the outside in, with his centerline well guarded by the elbow.

The motion and utilization of energy in chi sao is like that of a stream that is forever flowing without a moment of cessation or standing still. The "clinging stage" means "the mind stops to abide" —where it attaches itself to any object it encounters. Instead of flowing from one object to another, the mind stops with one.

In chi sao you simply feel and perceive the opponent's move; you do not allow your mind to stop with it; you move on just as you are toward the opponent and make use of his attack by turning it on to himself. As soon as your mind stops with an object of whatever nature—be it the opponent's technique or your own, the mode or the measure of the move—you cease to be master of yourself and are sure to fall victim to your opponent. When you set yourself *against* him, your mind will be carried away by him. Therefore, do not think of victory or even of yourself (understand the yin and yang as complementary instead of as opposition).

Kwan Yin, the goddess of mercy, is sometimes represented with 1,000 arms, each holding a different instrument. If her mind stops with the use, for instance, of a sword, all the other arms, 999 in number, will be of no use whatever. It is only because her mind doesn't stop with the use of one arm but moves from one instrument to another that all her arms prove useful with the utmost degree of efficiency.

For example, when I look at a tree, I perceive one of the leaves is red, and my mind stops with this leaf. When this happens, I see only one leaf and fail to take notice of the innumerable other leaves of the tree. If, instead of restricting my attention to one, I look at the tree without any preconceived ideas, I shall see all the leaves. One leaf effectively stops my mind from seeing all the rest. But when the mind moves on without stopping, it takes up hundreds of thousands of leaves without fail.

Therefore, as soon as there is a moment's stoppage your mind is no longer your own, for it is then placed under another's control. When the mind calculates so as to be quick in movement, the very thought makes the mind captive. When the ultimate perfection is attained in chi sao, the body and limbs perform by themselves what is assigned to them to do with no interference from the mind. The technical skill is so automatized it is completely divorced from conscious effort.

The next problem is where to keep the mind during sparring (i.e., chi-sao practice). When the mind is directed to the movements of the opponent, it is taken up by them. When it is directed to knock down the opponent, it is taken up by the idea of striking. When it is directed to defending yourself, it is taken up by the idea of defense.

Some martial artists suggest to keep the mind in the lower part of the abdomen just below the navel, and this will enable one to adjust oneself in accordance with the shifting of the situation from moment to moment. This is reasonable enough, and while being trained, the keeping of the mind in the lower region of the abdomen may not be a bad idea. But it is still the stage of reverence. After all, if you try to keep the mind imprisoned in the lower region of the abdomen, the very idea of keeping it in one specified locality will prevent the mind from operating anywhere else, and the result will be the contrary to what had been intended.

When you put your mind in the right hand, it will be kept captive in the right hand, and the rest of the body will be found inconvenienced. The result will be the same when you put it in the left hand or in the leg or in any other particular part of the body, because then the remaining parts of the body will feel its absence. The thing is not to *try* to localize the mind anywhere but to let if fill up the whole body, let it flow throughout the totality of your being. When this happens you use the hands when they are needed, and no time or no extra energy will be wasted. (The localization of the mind means it is freezing. When it ceases to flow freely as it is needed, it is no more the mind in its suchness.)

When the mind fills up the body entirely, it is said to be right; when it is located in any special part of the body, it is partial or one-sided. Chi sao dislikes partialization or localization. When the mind is not partialized after schematized plan, it naturally diffuses itself all over the body. It thus can meet the opponent as he moves about—trying to strike you down. When your hands are needed they are there to respond to your order. So with the legs—as they are needed. The mind never fails to operate them according to the situation. There is no need for the mind to maneuver itself out from any localized quarter (for example, lower abdomen) where it has been prearranged for it to station itself.

Do not localize your attention

Not to localize or partialize the mind is the end of spiritual training. When it is nowhere it is everywhere. When it occupies one tenth, it is absent in the other nine tenths. Let the gung fu man discipline himself to have the mind go on its own way, instead of trying deliberately to confine it somewhere. Therefore, during chi sao, you should have nothing purposely designed, nothing consciously calculated, no anticipation, no expectation. In short, you should be standing there like a dead man. To be conscious is characteristic of the human mind as distinguished from the mind of the lower animals. But when the mind becomes conscious of its doings, it ceases to be instinctual and its commands are colored with calculations and deliberations—which means that the connection between itself and the limbs is no longer direct because the identity of the commander and his executive agent is lost. When dualism (yang against yang) takes place, the whole personality never comes out as it is in *itself* (letting go itself from itself).

The empty-mindedness of chi sao applies to all activities we may perform, such as dancing. If the dancer has any idea at all of displaying his art well, he ceases to be a good dancer, for his mind stops with every movement he goes through. In all things, it is important to forget your mind and become one with the work at hand. When the mind is tied up, it feels inhibited in every move it makes and nothing will be accomplished with any sense of spontaneity. The wheel revolves when it is not too tightly attached to the axle. When it is too tight, it will never move on. As the Zen saying goes: "Into a soul absolutely free from thoughts and emotion, even the tiger finds no room to insert its fierce claws." In chi sao the mind is devoid of all fear, inferiority complexes, viscous feeling, etc., and is free from all forms of attachment, and it is master of itself, it knows no hindrances, no inhibitions, no stoppages, no clogging, no stickiness. It then follows its own course like water; it is like the wind that blows where it lists.

In the beginning, one naturally endeavors to do his best in gung fu, as in learning any other art. The technique has to be mastered. But as soon as his mind is fixed on anything, for instance if he desires to do well, or to display his skill, or to excel others, or if he is too anxiously bent on mastering his art, he is sure to commit more mistakes than are actually necessary. Why? Because his self-consciousness or ego-consciousness is too conspicuously present over the entire range of his attention—which fact interferes with a free display of whatever proficiency he has so far acquired or is going to acquire. He should get rid of this obtruding self—or ego-consciousness—and apply himself to the work to be done as if nothing particular were taking place at the moment. He should avoid:

1. The desire for victory
2. The desire to resort to technical cunning
3. The desire to display all that he has learned
4. The desire to play a passive role
5. The desire to get rid of whatever disease he is
   likely to be infected with

Things a gung fu man should do!

1. Give up thinking as though not giving it up. Observe the techniques as though not observing.

2. Having nothing left in your mind, keep it thoroughly cleansed of its contents, and then the mirror will reflect the images in their *isness*.

3. I am moving all day and not moving at all. I'm like the moon underneath the waves that ever goes on rolling and rocking. Let yourself go with the disease, be with it, keep company with it; this is the way to get rid of it.

4. You're said to have mastered the art of gung fu when the techniques work through your body and limbs as if independent of your conscious mind.

5. Turn yourself into a doll made of wood—it has no ego, it thinks nothing—and let the body and limbs work themselves out in accordance with the discipline they have undergone. This is the way to win.

6. Understand the interfusion of yin and yang, softness and firmness. Softness does not remain as such, nor does firmness.

They are always ready to change from one state to the other. This is the true fluidity of things, and the gung fu man should always be on the alert to meet this interchangeability of the opposites. But as soon as his mind stops with either of them, it loses its own fluidity. The gung fu man, therefore, should keep his mind always in the state of emptiness so that his freedom in action will never be obstructed.

The Tao of sticking hands

Chi sao, or sticking hands in gung fu, is the closest to Taoism and Zen. This art aims at harmony with the practitioner and his opponent. It's principle follows the Taoist principle of wu wei. Wu means "not" or "non" and wei means "action," "striving," "straining," or "busyness." It doesn't really mean doing nothing, but to let one's mind alone, trusting it to work by itself. Wu wei, in gung fu, means mind-action, in the sense that the governing force is the mind and not that of the senses. During sparring, a gung fu man learns to forget about himself and follows the movements of his opponent, leaving his mind free to make its own counter-movement without any interference or deliberation.

In sticking hands, a gung fu man frees himself from all mental suggestions of resistance, and adopts a supple attitude. His actions are all performed without self-assertion; he lets his mind remain spontaneous and ungrasped. Every action is activated by those of the opponent's. He does not resist or give way completely, but is as pliable as a spring.

Because of the self there is the foe; when there is no self there is no foe. The foe means an opposition as the male is opposed to the female and fire to water. Whatever things have form exist necessarily in opposition. When there are no signs (of thought movement) stirred in your mind, no conflicts of opposition take place there, and when there are no conflicts, one trying to get the better of the other, this is known as "neither opponent nor self." When, further, the mind itself is forgotten together with signs (of thought movement), you enjoy a state of absolutely doing-nothingness, you are in a state of perfectly quiet passivity, you're in harmony with the world, you are *one with it*. While the foe-form ceases to exist, you're not conscious of it. Your mind is cleansed of all thought movement, and you act only when there is a prompting (from the unconscious).

Sticking hands is just like the nature of water: Water is so fine that it is impossible to grasp a handful of it; strike it yet it does not suffer hurt; stab it and it is not wounded. Like water, a gung fu man has no shape or technique of his own, but molds or fits his movement into that of his opponent's. It is true that water is the weakest substance in the world, yet when it attacks it can go through the hardest. It can be calm like a still pond and turbulent like the Niagara Falls.

Objectivity and subjectivity are obscurely grasped together. It is the *nondifferentiating* awareness of the fact that statements such as "this is also that; that is also this," and "destruction is construction; construction is destruction" are meaningless. There is no destruction or construction. They fuse into one. When we do not assert either action or nonaction, this or that, being or nonbeing, we are free from both.

The Tao of Gung Fu

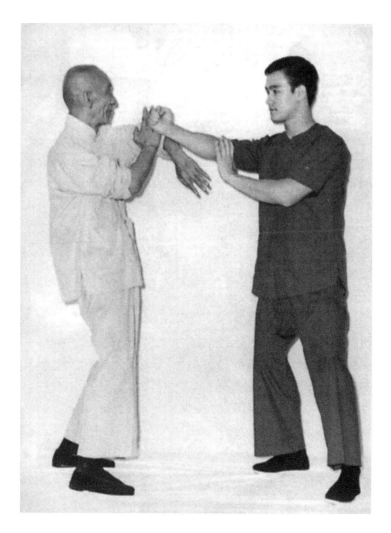

The path of nonassertion

The understanding of chi sao is an inner experience in which distinction between self and opponent vanishes. It is an intuitive, immediate awareness rather than a mediated, inferential, or intellectual process. While the action of assertion, man's common tendency, is preconceptual and rational, it cannot penetrate the hidden recesses of creativity. The action of assertion is viewed from the externals of intellection, while the action of nonassertion is activated by the inner light. The former action is limited and finite, the latter free and limitless.

Chi sao factors that all martial artists should consider

In chi sao, as you are rotating your arms up and down in semi-circular arcs, it is crucial to follow your partner's movements as closely as possible and to maintain the correct hand position throughout the exercise. The chi sao rotation pattern resembles the arcs the arms would take if turning the oversize steering wheel of a large bus. Try to keep your elbows close throughout the movement and never allow them to come closer than three inches to your stomach. Also consider the following:

1. The techniques
2. Sticking hands combined with close-range tactics
3. Countering sticking hands
4. Training aids

Chi sao techniques to be practiced

1. Tying up your opponent's hands by crossing them
2. Striking up the center
3. Striking to the outside
4. Striking below the arms
5. Chi sao to backfist
6. Chi sao to straight punch
7. Chi sao to chop choy
8. Chi sao to peacock eye

GUNG FU KICKING TECHNIQUES

It is important when attempting to initiate kicking in gung fu to keep your kicks low. In training, it is okay to kick as high as you can, but in actual combat it is more important to kick as fast as you can and never let your kick pass above the belt area. It is too easy to be knocked or set off balance by such sudden tilting of the torso and legs. Your kicks should also correspond with your hand techniques (i.e., simple, direct, and efficient without ornamentation or attempts at sophisticated movement).

It is also important that your kicking foot snap back immediately after landing your kick and do not attempt high or flying kicks in a real fight. If you can be put off balance easily simply performing a standing kick, you will be totally off balance for any type of aerial maneuver.

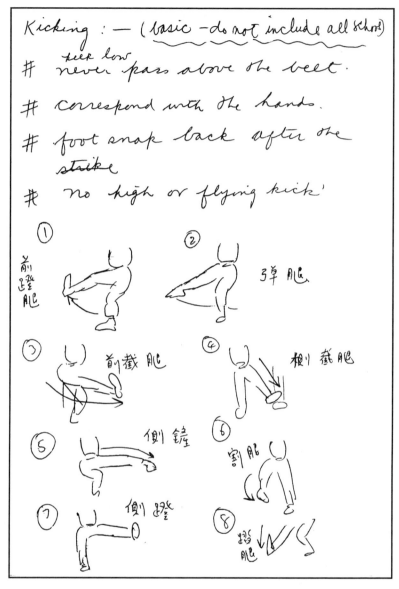

Kicking techniques to practice

1. Classic Wing Chun kicking techniques (i.e., heel kick, rear heel kick, and low side kick with the edge of the foot)
2. High double kick (used only for practicing flexibility—*not* to be used in real-life encounters)
3. Low step-over side kick

Figure 1. B attempts to strike A with a right hook.

Figure 2. A directs B's punch up and outside while simultaneously delivering a front kick to B's groin.

Figure I

Figure 2

Figure 3

Figure 4

The high double kick (Figures I and 2)—in which one kicks as high as possible with one leg, then, while the kicking leg is coming down, one executes a second high kick with the opposite leg—along with the high front kick (Figure 3) and high hook kick (Figure 4), are great practice techniques to enhance your flexibility. But they have limited practical value in self-defense situations.

The Tao of Gung Fu

Figure 1

Figure 2

Figure 3

Figure 4

Figures 1 and 2. Making sure that 80 percent of your weight is on your rear or support-
ing leg, you can quickly shoot out a front kick, using the sole or heel of your foot to strike
the stomach of your opponent. Using higher kicks, such as the side kick and hook kick
(Figures 3 and 4, respectively), in practice will help to give you a feel for kicking and en-
hance the balance and coordination skills needed to kick effectively.

Some Techniques of Gung Fu

SELF-DEFENSE CONSIDERATIONS

What would you do if you were attacked by a thug? Would you stand your ground and fight it out? Or, if you will excuse me, would you say that you would run like hell? But what if your loved ones were with you? What then? That's the all-important question.

You have only to pick up a newspaper to read of attacks made, not only on lonely commons, but also in built-up areas, to understand the need for self-defense. "To be forewarned is to be forearmed" is an old, reliable proverb, and the purpose of my notes on self-defense is not only to forewarn you, but to forearm you with a practical knowledge of meeting any foe, regardless of his size and strength.

Self-defense is not fun. You are liable to find yourself fighting hard to avoid serious injury and so you must expect to be hurt. The method of self-defense I am going to describe will not prevent your being hurt but will give you a very good chance of emerging the victor without any severe injury. You will have to accept this and should a blow from your opponent break through it is essential—at least for the time being—to ignore the pain caused and, instead of giving up, use it as something to spur on your counter-attack and victory.

Bear this in mind: When being attacked by a thug, the fact is that he has but a one-track mind which is bent on your destruction, rarely considering what you can do, and if your acts show him that he is up against something he did not expect, it will cut down his attacking ego over 50 percent and will neutralize his attack, in which case you always have the psychological advantage on your side.

This may not sound very encouraging, but the chances of attack can be very greatly reduced if you are walking, especially alone, at night or in lonely places, if you are always alert. Keep an eye on any person who appears to be following you or who approaches. Keep to the outside of the path or in the middle of a lane. Listen for approaching footsteps and watch shadows; that is to say, as you pass a street lamp you will see the shadow of anyone behind you thrown up on the ground in front of you. The same thing happens as the result of lights in houses and the headlamps of passing cars. As soon as you see a shadow in these circumstances, immediately glance around and see who it is. Always, of course, avoid patches of deep shadow.

In made-up but quiet streets, I repeat, walk on the outside of the pavement. This obviates the chance of anyone jumping out of a house or garden entrance at you to snatch your purse, handbag, briefcase, or worse. For exactly the same reason I suggest walking down the middle of a lane where there are no made-up paths and perhaps no street lamps. If you consider it advisable, you can even cross the road to avoid a person of whom you are suspicious. If he follows, he at least makes his intention fairly obvious. Although I am again repeating myself, I must emphasize that the success of an assailant's attack depends on surprise, and if you're sufficiently alert to prevent a surprise, your counterattack is already halfway to being successful. The main thing is to see the attack coming, which enables you to shout, scream, or just concentrate on dealing with the attacker. It is also advisable to make as much noise as possible as this naturally tends to frighten off lawbreakers.

I hope I have not frightened you and made you think it is not safe to walk along the streets. That is certainly not my intention, but newspaper reports lead one to believe that attacks on innocent people are increasing.

The Tao of Gung Fu

The special features of employing gung fu in self-defense situations is that every movement has a flowing continuity without any dislocation; defense is attack, attack is defense, each being the cause and result of the other. Its techniques are smooth, short, and extremely fast; they are direct, to the point, and are stripped down to their essential purposes without any wasted motions. Simplicity is the key word in this art—to do the utmost in the minimum of motion and energy and can be practiced by both sexes.

The average person is usually over-impressed by the size and arrogance of his possible opponent who usually uses his thuggish arrogance for all it is worth, seeking to create an effective bluff to frighten or subordinate your resistance to his apparent superior size and brutal grimaces, neither of which are positive proof of his ability to subdue you. He works on the common idea that a smaller person is usually scared by his size—but don't be fooled. Pay absolutely no attention to his size, his arrogance, fierce facial contortions, nor his viscous language. They are just psychological aspects that are no criterion as to his actual strength and combat efficiency. They have been effective factors but are no more to those who are willing to learn the value of the old axiom—"The bigger they are, the harder they fall."

Size is never a true indication of muscular power and efficiency, as all Chinese boxing masters know only too well. The smaller man usually makes up for the balance of power by his greater agility, flexibility, speed of foot, and nervous action. Bear this in mind once you go into action and fight with your opponent at his weakest points of vantage which are mainly gravitation, throwing him off balance, and applying such leverage principles so that his body is used toward his own defeat. Also bear in mind that once you hesitate, or stop, the stronger person has the chance to bring his strength to bear, but never if you keep moving, and are particularly faster than he.

The only one point to bear in mind when being attacked by a thug is the fact that the thug has but a one-track mind. He thinks in but one groove, which is bent on your destruction, rarely considering what you can do. If your act and attitude instantly show your opponent that he is up against something he did not expect, it will cut down his attacking ego over 50 percent, causing him either to stop his intended attack or even turn tail—in which case you always can relax.

Some self-defense techniques

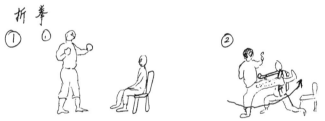

Figure 1. Opponent B moves in to kick A while A is seated in a chair. Figure 2. A blocks B's kick with a kwun sao, or flopping-hand block, while simultaneously delivering a straight punch to his opponent's midsection.

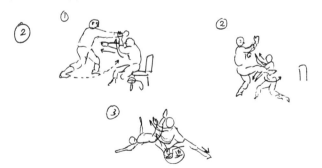

Figure 1. Opponent B attacks A with a right punch, which A blocks with an outside, high rear block while simultaneously delivering a punch to B's ribs. Figure 2. B delivers a kick to A (now standing), which A blocks with a low, outer wrist block (goang sao) while pushing his right palm toward B's chest. Figure 3. Hooking his right heel behind B's right heel, A pushes B over.

The Tao of Gung Fu

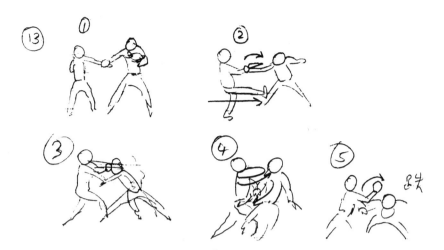

Figure 1. B grabs A by the left wrist. Figure 2. A immediately pivots to face B, grabbing B's wrist with lop sao and simultaneously delivering a right-heel kick to B's knee. Figure 3. A then delivers a left straight punch to B's face. Figures 4 and 5. A follows up the straight punch with a left-hand lop sao and back fist (gwa choi) technique.

Figure 1. B attempts a left punch against A. Figure 2. A blocks with an outside high rear block while simultaneously striking B's chest with a knuckle strike. Figure 3. B attempts a right punch, which is blocked by A using a left open-hand block, which A instantly converts to a pulling hand (lop sao) and right straight punch. Figures 4 and 5. A swings his right foot in between B's feet and executes a foot sweep. As soon as B hits the ground, A finishes him off with a punch to the head.

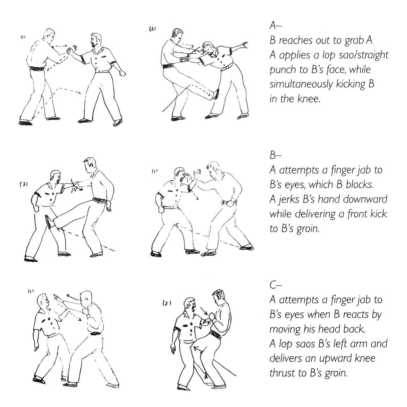

A—
B reaches out to grab A
A applies a lop sao/straight punch to B's face, while simultaneously kicking B in the knee.

B—
A attempts a finger jab to B's eyes, which B blocks. A jerks B's hand downward while delivering a front kick to B's groin.

C—
A attempts a finger jab to B's eyes when B reacts by moving his head back. A lop saos B's left arm and delivers an upward knee thrust to B's groin.

Two counter-offensive actions—the stop hit and the time hit

In any form of attack, the final choice of stroke should be based on the observation of your opponent's reactions, habits, and preferences. Thus, observe, deduce, and apply. The three factors influencing a successful attack are a fine sense of timing, a perfect judgment of distance, and a correct application of cadence. Therefore, if you can act so as to disturb your opponent's rhythm by causing him to lose a period of gung fu time, you will better your chances for success.

A good gung fu man should develop great mobility and acquire a fine sense of distance, learning how to break ground effectively. His stance should be slightly shorter in order to keep the leading leg and foot out of range of a sudden kick and his mobility or breaking of ground should be accomplished by small and rapid steps. Factors such as distance should be governed by the amount of target to be protected and the parts of the body that are most easily within the adversary's reach. You must be able to advance or retire before, while, or after the strike or kick at which you are working has been executed.

Two tremendously effective counter-offensive actions are the stop hit and the time hit, both of which make the adversary respect his distance.

The stop hit

The stop hit is a counter defense/offense against an opponent who attacks wildly, with insufficient care to protect himself, or who comes too close.

The time hit

The time hit requires one to do the following:

1. The final line in which the attack is delivered must be anticipated.

2. The executant must be covered (protected).

3. The timing of the stroke must be perfect.

The leading right shin/knee stop kick

When your opponent attacks you, he has to come to you, and this action of coming toward you offers you the opportunity to apply the theory of attack just outlined. It is always wise to use the longest weapon against the nearest target. When your opponent advances toward you, he presents to you his "advanced target" of his shin and knee. Before his attack is halfway through, you can stop kick him and thus, check his attack.

1. A and B facing each other

2. Awareness is most important in the success of any stop hit or kick, though the stop kick is easier, allowing the defender more time due to the longer kicking distance between him and his opponent. The second A is aware of B's initial on-slaught, A immediately shoots out his shin/knee stop kick while arching back for more power and a safer distance.

The side kick

The longest of all kicks, this side/rear kick can be a strong defensive weapon, especially against all-hand attacks, round-house kicking, or rear leg attacks of the opponent.

The hook kick

The hook kick is a good counter-kick, especially against a hand attack.

The finger jab

The straight finger jab (biu jee) is used when the opponent attempts to strike, bringing his hand out of the centerline. This finger jab can also be successfully used against an opponent who feints, or swings wildly. It is a simple but practical technique; you will be amazed how a simple finger jab like this can interrupt and upset your opponent's fancy mess.

THE PRACTICE OF FORMS— ONE OF THE MEANS TO AN END

Gung fu can be practiced alone or with a partner. Practicing alone involves the use of forms, a series of combative movements that are performed and practiced in succession. There are all kinds of forms in gung fu, many of which are based on the combative movements of animals, such as the crane, the monkey, the praying mantis, and so on.

Some postures from the Tiger (Figure 1, left) and Crane (Figure 2, right) forms of Chinese gung fu.

The method of practicing forms should be very fluid as you transition from one movement or technique to another. This is based on the old gung fu principle "flowing water as running water never grows stale." Apart from the cultivation of proper body alignment and delivery of techniques, the practice of forms is not all that strenuous. Such nonstrenuous exercise serves to normalize—instead of overdeveloping or overexerting—the body.

Wing Chun's sil lum tao

A great form (particularly the first third) for learning most of the defensive positions needed for the effective application of Wing Chun gung fu is the sil lum tao (or little imagination). It is impor-

Figure 1

Figure 2

Figure 3

Some postures from sil lum tao. Tan sao (palm-up) block (Figure 1) and jun sao (Figure 2) sinking arm block are just two of the 108 movements required of this form. There are three sections, the first third of which involves iso-tension movements performed slowly in order to develop proper neuromuscular efficiency in striking, blocking, and protecting the centerline. Other forms in gung fu emphasize such things as the square stance (Figure 3), which is considered one of the more elementary postures in gung fu.

tant when performing this form to keep your elbows in toward the center, with your arms in a state of semicontraction, and the forearms level when in the lower positions.

Some postures from wu-shu; an example of a classical Chinese martial art form.

Further examples of some forms practiced in gung fu.

The Tao of Gung Fu

Walking along the bank of Lake Washington

The breeze on the bank
Already blows cool and mild;

The distant merging of lake and sky
Is but a red trace of sunset.

The deep silence of the lake
Cuts off all tumult from me.

Along the lonely bank
I move with slow footsteps:

Alone the disturbed frogs scurry off.

Here and there are houses,
Cool beads of light spring out from them.

A dazzling moon shines down
from the lonely depths of the sky.

In the moonlight
Slowly I move to a gung fu form.

Body and soul are fused into one.

Some Techniques of Gung Fu

A GUNG FU TRAINING PROGRAM

The following is a suggested gung fu training program for students.

Limbering exercises

Limbering or warm-up exercises are a must in the general program to strengthen and to enhance flexibility prior to technique training. The main parts of the body that should be warmed up are:

1. *The waist*—the waist can best be warmed up by performing exercises such as twisting, bending to the front, back, left, and right, and by rotating the hips.

2. *The legs*—the best exercises to employ for limbering up the legs are mainly stretching or high kicking exercises. If you choose high kicking, focus on the front kick and the side kick.

3. *The shoulders*—an efficient warm-up for the shoulders would involve wide arm circles or rotations and pulling back with your arms so that a mild stretch of the shoulder girdle is achieved.

4. *The arms*—the best warm-up for the arms would be mainly exercises such as push-ups or any basic weight-training exercise (such as barbell curls) which have proven beneficial.

5. *The wrist*—the most efficient warm-up for the wrists is simply rotating them in clockwise and counterclockwise circles. You can also contract or flex the extensor muscles in your forearms against resistance with exercises such as a seated wrist curl or standing reverse barbell curl with weight.

The important thing with regard to training is to use your own ideas based on what you think you need (e.g., increased flexibility in your hips, waist, shoulders, etc.). Think constantly about creating new ways to improve the functioning of your body in the art of gung fu and the hell with conventional methods and opinions.

Technique training

It is important to practice partner facing in your workouts. If you can keep your nose facing that of your partner/opponent as he maneuvers around the room, you will develop more proficiency in guarding and maintaining your centerline.

In practicing techniques such as punching and kicking, I have found the following apparatus to be useful in gung fu training:

1. A large, hanging heavy bag
2. A small striking pad on a pine board
3. A hanging wall bag
4. A small hanging bag
5. Iron rings
6. A sand dish
7. A mook jong (wooden dummy)
8. A stationary striking ball
9. A single-head staff
10. A pair of handgrips
11. A pair of dumbbells
12. A skipping rope

Some classical gung fu equipment and their uses

The wooden dummy

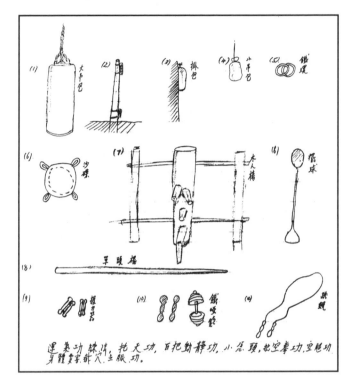

One unique but useful piece of training equipment I use is the portable wooden dummy. I use the dummy to develop power and better techniques. The dummy is approximately six feet tall and twelve inches in diameter. It is erected upon an eight foot by eight foot platform and supported by a metal spring. The dummy has two portable hands below the neck and another in the center. They stretch out about two feet. The hands are constructed loosely and are removable. The dummy also has one metal leg that extends out and downward.

I make use of the dummy's hands to practice blocks and punches and also for techniques in sticking hands. The dummy will never replace a live sparring mate, but it is very useful for blocking and pulling techniques which can be done with full force as the dummy cannot be damaged. It is also useful in teaching one to punch straight. The dummy's foot is also beneficial in teaching the martial artist to always place his front leg automatically to lock or obstruct his opponent's leg, thus preventing him from kicking. It is also valuable for practicing shin kicks.

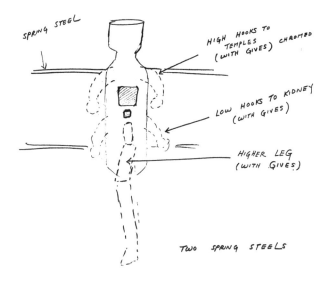

The square wall bag

Another piece of apparatus that I find very helpful in my gung fu training is the square wall bag filled with beans, which develops depth and penetration techniques. It also gives a feeling of hitting someone. It is a wonderful training apparatus to develop wrist strength for perfecting your straight punching technique. The bag should be mounted against a wall at approximately nose level. The wall bag is very effective in developing impact power in your punching techniques, however, it is not an end itself as too much wall bag punching can retard your speed.

Air punching/kicking

Balancing out your power training should be speed training. The technique of throwing punches without actually making contact (i.e., air punching) is utilized to develop speed in your techniques. I should caution you, however, that too much air punching could possibly damage the elbow or cause tendonitis.

The hanging paper

The hanging paper is a good exercise to develop precision in your straight punching. Hang a sheet of paper (8 x 10) from the ceiling (preferably by a chain so that it returns instantly to a vertical position after you strike it) and then punch at it with a series of straight punches in rapid succession It should help you to develop snap and impact power in your techniques.

Iron rings

For better results in sil lum tao, I advocate using iron rings on one's forearms while doing tan sao (palm-up block) and fook sao (palm-down, bent-arm, elbow-in block), as the weight gives the actual resistance of the opponent's arm pressing on you. Instead of pure imagination, a real feeling is being felt on the arms as they slowly go outward from the body. The main point is that with the weights on your wrist— as opposed to simply holding a dumbbell—you can keep your fingers and wrists relaxed, as they

need to be in chi sao. I showed the iron rings method (I've made four pairs, at three pounds each) to my instructor in Wing Chun, Yip Man, and he is convinced when I demonstrated to him that in sil lum tao, when the tan sao is coming out, it is supposed to be going into a fook sao, and when a fook sao is coming out, it is supposed to stop the oncoming. Thus, the iron rings will give the necessary resistance when the practitioner directs his energy outward without tensing his fingers and wrists. Further, as one progresses along in his training, more and more resistance can be provided by simply wearing more iron rings on one's arms. This is an alive way of building without getting the hands rigid. This is a kind of modernized progressive weight-training method that is effective.

Make use of the wooden dummy and some of the other equipment I've mentioned above in your own gung fu training. Constantly come up with new ways and means to better your training results.

My personal gung fu training program

1. Punching

   a. *Air punching—3 sets of 50 each*

   b. *Sand plate—3 sets of 50 each*

   c. *Hanging bag—3 sets of 50 each*

2. Kicking

   a. *Leg stretching*

   • *Forward stretch—3 sets of 12 each*

   • *Side stretch—3 sets of 12 each*

   b. *Straight kick—3 sets of 12 each*

   c. *Side kick—3 sets of 12 each*

   d. *Kicking form*

3. Wooden dummy

   a. *The classical form of 108*

   b. *Individual technique training*

   c. *Training in entering*

4. Form practice

   • *Sil lum tao, hand techniques, and Wing Chun fist*

5. Individual technique practice

6. Sticking hand training

7. Freestyle practice

Program for Bruce J. F. Lee

Training Program - 訓練表 -

(一) Punching- 拳切 -

    (a) Air punching- 空拳 -   3 times of 50 each.
    (b) Sand plate--- 沙碟 -   3 times of 50 each.
    (c) Hanging bag- 吊包 -   3 times of 50 each.

(二) Kicking- 踢腿

    (a) Leg stretching- 压腿
        (1) forward stretch- 正 3 times of 12 each.
        (2) side   stretch- 侧 3 times of 12 each.
    (b) Straight kick- 直撑 3 times of 12 each.
    (c) Side kick--- 侧 " 3 times of 12 each.
    (d) Kicking form 腿術 3 times each.

(三) Wooden Dummy- 木人樁

    (a) The classical Form of 108. 一百〇八樁手 -
    (b) Individual technique training. 單式練污 -
    (c) Training in entering. 入樁污 -

(四) Form practice 一 拳術 訓 練 (一) 小念頭 (二) 詠春拳.

(五) Individual technique practice 單式 对 練 -

(六) Sticking hand training. 黐手

(七) Free style practice 無限條自由搏擊

Additional technique training to consider

A. 1. Finger jab

    2. Trap and hit

    3. Pak sao and straight blast

    4. Inside pak sao and strike to opponent's right side

    5. Lop sao

B. 1. Pak sao

    2. Lop sao

    3. Backfist

    4. Straight punch to backfist (left and right)

5. Pak sao to backfist

6. Double lop sao

7. Low hit to backfist

8. Low hit to backfist to kick

9. Hit on inside gate

10. Inside gate straight blast

11. Hit low to backfist

Classical techniques

1. Pak sao

2. Lop sao

3. Backfist

4. Low strike to backfist (left and right)

5. Pak sao to backfist

6. Double lop sao and backfist

7. Low punch to backfist, lop sao to backfist

8. Jut sao (pull down opponent's guard and hit)

9. Low strike to backfist to kick

10. Attacking inside gate

11. Inside gate to low backfist

12. Inside kick to straight blast

Wooden dummy techniques

1. The yun jeong (vertical palm strike)

2. The jik chung (vertical fist strike—you should add a foam rubber covering to the striking area of the dummy to practice this technique effectively)

3. The bong sao (high elbow block)

4. The tawn sao (palm up block)

5. The fook sao (bent-arm elbow-in block)

6. The gong sao (low outer wrist block)

Combination techniques

1. Shin kick with pak sao and straight punch

2. Finger jab to low groin strike to straight punch

3. Rear leg kick and finger jab

4. Feint kick to finger jab to straight blast

The major thing to remember when training is not the number of moves that you practice, but how well you learn and develop each move. It is better to do two things effectively than to do a hundred things poorly.

Part 3

TAOISM IN THE CHINESE ART OF GUNG FU

THE TAO OF GUNG FU

Gung fu is more than just an excellent physical exercise or a highly scientific method of self-defense. To the Chinese, gung fu is a Way of training the mind as well as a Way of life. The spiritual side of gung fu cannot be learned by fact-finding or instruction in facts. It has to grow spontaneously, like a flower, in a mind free from desires and emotions. The core of this principle of gung fu is Tao—the spontaneity of the universe.

The philosophy of the Tao is called Taoism and is expressed chiefly through the writings of Lao-tzu in his book, *The Tao Te Ching (The Book of the Way)*. The philosophy of Taoism reveals the essential unity of the universe (monism)—or reversion, polarization (yin/yang), and eternal cycles—of the leveling of all differences, the relativity of all standards, and the return of all to the primeval oneness, the divine intelligence, the source of all things. From this naturally arises the absence of desire for strife and contention and fighting for advantage. Thus, the teachings of humility and meekness of the Christian "Sermon on the Mount" find a rational basis and a peaceable temper is bred in man. It emphasizes nonresistance and the importance of gentleness.

The basic idea of the *Tao Te Ching* is naturalism in the sense of wu-wei (nondoing), which really means taking no unnatural action. It means spontaneity; that is, "to support all things in their natural stage" and thus allow them to "transform spontaneously." In this manner Tao "undertakes no activity and yet there is nothing left undone." In ordinary life it is expressed in "producing and rearing things without taking possession of them" and "doing work but not taking pride in it"—thus the natural Way stands in complement to all artificial ways such as regulation, ceremonies, etc. This is the reason why the Taoists don't like formalities and artificiality.

The natural Way is compared with the ways of water. The female and the infant; that is, the way of the weak. While there seems to be glorification of the weak, the strongest stress really lies with simplicity. A simple life is one of plainness in which profit is discarded, cleverness abandoned, selfishness eliminated, and desires reduced. It is the life of "perfection which seems to be incomplete and of fullness which seems to be empty." It is the life which is as bright as light but does not dazzle. In short, it is a life of harmony, unity, contentment, tranquillity, constancy, enlightenment, peace, and long life.

The word *Tao* has no exact equivalent in the English language. To render it into *Way, principle,* or *law* is to give it too narrow an interpretation. Lao-tzu, the founder of Taosim, described Tao in the following words:

> The Way which can be expressed in words is not the eternal
> Way; the Name which can be uttered is not the eternal Name.
> Conceived of as nameless, it is the cause of heaven and earth.
> Conceived of as having a name, it is the mother of all things.
> Only the man eternally free from passion can contemplate its
> spiritual essence. He who is clogged by desires can see no more
> than its outer form. These two things, the spiritual (yin) and
> the material (yang), though we call them by different names,
> are one and the same in their origin. The sameness is a mystery
> of the mysteries. It is the gate of all that is subtle and wonderful.

In *Masterpieces of World Philosophy*

> Tao is the nameless beginning of things, the universal
> principle underlying everything, the supreme, ultimate
> pattern, and the principle of growth.

Huston Smith, the author of *World Religion,* explained Tao as:

The Way of Ultimate Reality—the Way or Principle behind all life, or the Way man should order his life to gear in with the way the universe operates.

Although no one word can substitute its meaning, I have used the word *Truth* for it—the Truth behind gung fu; the Truth that every gung fu practitioner should follow.

Yin and yang

Tao operates in yin and yang, a pair of mutually complementary forces that are at work in and behind all phenomena. This principle of yin/yang, also known as t'ai chi, is the basic structure of gung fu. However, as I've gone into detail about yin/yang elsewhere in this book, I will simply refer you to Chapter Two for additional information on this very important principle.

Applied yin–yang: the Law of Harmony

The application of the theory of yin–yang in gung fu is known as the Law of Harmony, in which one should be in harmony with, and not in opposition to, the strength and force of the opposition. This means that one should do nothing that is not natural or spontaneous; the important thing is not to strain in any way. Suppose opponent A applies force on opponent B; B should not give way to it (for these are the two extreme opposites of B's reaction to A's force). Instead, B should complete A's force with a lesser force (firmness in gentleness) and lead him to the direction of his own force and movement. This spontaneous assisting of A's movement as he aims it will result in his own defeat. As the butcher preserves his knife by cutting along the bone and not against it, a gung fu man preserves himself by following the movement of his opponent without opposition.

Therefore gentleness alone can't forever dissolve away great force, nor sheer brute force to subdue one's foe. In order to survive

in combat, the harmonious interfusion of gentleness and firmness is necessary; with one sometimes dominating the other and vice versa, in a wavelike succession. The movement will then truly flow; for the true fluidity of movement is in its interchangeability. This is also true in life.

The Law of Noninterference with Nature

The above idea gives rise to a closely related law, the Law of Non-interference with Nature, which teaches a gung fu man to forget about himself and follow his opponent (strength) instead of himself; he does not move ahead but responds to the fitting influence. The basic idea is to defeat the opponent by yielding to him and using his own strength against him. That is why a gung fu man never asserts himself against his opponent, and never puts himself in frontal opposition to the direction of his force. When being attacked, he will not resist, but will control the attack by swinging with it. This law illustrates the principles of nonresistance and nonviolence, which were founded on the idea that the branches of a fir tree snapped under the weight of the snow, while the simple reeds, weaker but more supple, can overcome it. In the *I' Ching,* Confucius illustrated this: "To stand in the stream is a datum of nature; one must follow and flow with it."

In *Tao Te Ching,* the gospel of Taoism, Lao-tzu pointed out to us the value of gentleness. Contrary to common belief, the yin principle, as softness and pliableness, is to be associated with life and survival. Because he can yield, a man can survive. In contrast, the yang principle, which is assumed to be rigorous and hard, makes a man break under pressure (note the last two lines, which make a fair description of revolution as many generations of people have seen it):

> Alive, a man is supple, soft,
> In death, unbending, rigorous.
> All creatures, grass and trees, alive are plastic but are pliant too,
> And dead, are friable and dry.
> Unbending rigor is the mate of death,
> And yielding softness, company of life.
> Unbending soldiers get no victories;
> The stiffest tree is readiest for the ax.
> The strong and mighty topple from their place;
> The soft and yielding rise above them all.

The way of movement in gung fu is closely related to the movement of the mind. In fact, the mind is trained to direct the movement of the body. The mind wills and the body behaves. As the mind is to direct the bodily movements, the way to control the mind is important; but it is not an easy task. In his book *Power in Athletics,* Glen Clark mentioned some of the emotional disturbances in athletics:

> Every conflicting center, every extraneous, disrupting, decentralizing emotion, jars the natural rhythm and reduces a man's efficiency on the gridiron far more seriously than physical jars and bodily conflicts can ever jar him. The

emotions that destroy the inner rhythm of a man are hatred, jealousy, lust, envy, pride, vanity, covetousness, and fear.

To perform the right technique in gung fu, physical loosening must be continued in a mental and spiritual loosening, so as to make the mind free and agile. In order to accomplish this, a gung fu man has to remain quiet and calm and to master the principle of no-mindedness (wu-hsin).

ON WU-HSIN
(NO-MINDEDNESS)

The phenomenon of wu-hsin, or "no-mindedness," is not a blank mind that shuts out all thoughts and emotions; nor is it simply calmness and quietness of mind.

Although quietude and calmness are necessary, it is the "non-graspingness" of thoughts that mainly constitutes the principle of no mind. A gung fu man employs his mind as a mirror—it grasps nothing and refuses nothing; it receives but does not keep. As Allan Watts puts it, the no-mindedness is:

> A state of wholeness in which the mind functions freely and easily, without the sensation of a second mind or ego standing over it with a club.

What he means is: Let the mind think what it likes without interference by the separate thinker or ego within oneself. So long as it thinks what it wants, there is absolutely no effort in letting it go; and the disappearance of the effort to let go is precisely the disappearance of the separate thinker. There is nothing to try to do, for whatever comes up moment by moment is accepted, including nonacceptance. No-mindedness is, then, not being without emotion or feeling, but being one in whom feeling is not sticky or blocked. It is a mind immune to emotional influences.

Like this river, everything is flowing on ceaselessly without cessation or standing still.

No-mindedness is to employ the whole mind as we use the eyes when we rest them upon various objects but make no special effort to take anything in. Chuang-tzu, the disciple of Lao-tzu, stated:

The baby looks at things all day without winking, that is because his eyes are not focused on any particular object. He goes without knowing where he is going, and stops without knowing what he is doing. He merges himself with the surroundings and moves along with it. These are the principles of mental hygiene.

Therefore, concentration in gung fu does not have the usual sense of restricting the attention to a single sense object, but is simply a quiet awareness of whatever happens to be here and now. Such concentration can be illustrated by an audience at a football game; instead of a concentrated attention on the player that has the ball, they have an awareness of the whole football field. In a similar way, a gung fu man's mind is concentrated by not dwelling on any particular part of the opponent. This is especially true when dealing with many opponents. For instance, suppose ten men are attacking him, each in succession ready to strike him down. As soon as one is disposed of, he will move on to another without permitting the mind to stop with any. However rapidly one blow may follow another, he leaves no time to intervene between the two. Everyone of the ten will thus be successively and successfully dealt with. This is possible only when the mind moves from one object to another without being stopped or arrested by anything. If the mind is unable to move on in this fashion, it is sure to lose the combat somewhere between two encounters.

His mind is present everywhere because it is nowhere attached to any particular object. And it can remain present because
even when related to this or that object, it does not cling to it. The
flow of thought is like water filling a pond, which is always ready to
flow off again. It can work its inexhaustible power because it is free,
and be open to everything because it is empty. This can be compared with what Chang Chen Chi called "serene reflection." He
wrote:

> Serene means tranquillity of no thought, and reflection
> means vivid and clear awareness. Therefore, serene reflection
> is clear awareness of no-thought.

As stated earlier, a gung fu man aims at harmony with himself
and his opponent. It also stated that harmony with one's opponent
is possible not through force, which provokes conflicts and reactions, but through a yielding to his force. In other words, a gung fu
man promotes the spontaneous development of his opponent and
does not venture to interfere by his own action. He loses himself

by giving up all subjective feelings and individuality, and becomes one with his opponent. Inside his mind oppositions have become mutually cooperative instead of mutually exclusive. When his private ego and conscious efforts yield to a power not his own he then achieves the supreme action, nonaction (wu wei).

ON WU-WEI
(NONDOING)

Wu means "not" or "non" and wei means "action," "doing," "striving," "straining" or "busyness." It doesn't really mean doing nothing, but to let one's mind alone, trusting it to work by itself. Wu wei, in gung fu, means spontaneous action or spirit-action, in the sense that the governing force is the mind and not that of the senses. During sparring, a gung fu man learns to forget about himself and follows the movement of his opponent, leaving his mind free to make it's own counter-movement without any interfering deliberation. He frees himself from all mental suggestions of resistance, and adopts a supple attitude. His actions are all performed without self-assertion; he lets his mind remain spontaneous and ungrasped. As soon as he stops to think, his flow of movement will be disturbed and he is immediately struck by his opponent. Every action, therefore, has to be done "unintentionally" without ever trying.

Through wu wei, a reposeful ease is secured. This passive achievement, as Chuang-tzu pointed out, will free a gung fu man from striving and straining himself.

A yielding will has a resposeful ease, soft as downy feathers, a quietude, a shrinking from action, an appearance of inability to do. Placidly free from anxiety, one acts with the opportune time; one moves and revolves in the line of creation. One does not move ahead but responds to the fitting influences. Establish nothing in regard to oneself. Let things be what they are, move like water, rest like a mirror, respond like an echo, pass quickly like the nonexistent and be quiet as purity. Those who gain, lose. Do not precede others, always follow them.

The natural phenomenon which the gung fu man sees as being the closest resemblance to wu wei is water:

Nothing is weaker than water,
But when it attacks something hard,
Or resistant, then nothing withstands it,
And nothing will alter its way.

The above passages from the *Tao Te Ching* illustrate to us the nature of water: Water is so fine that it is impossible to grasp a handful of it; strike it, yet it does not suffer hurt; stab it, and it is not wounded; sever it, and yet it is not divided. It has no shape of its own, but molds itself to the receptacle that contains it. When heated to the state of steam it is invisible, but has enough power to split the earth itself. When frozen it crystallizes into a mighty rock. First it is turbulent like the Niagara Falls, and then calm like a still pond, fearful like a torrent, and refreshing like a spring on a hot summer's day. So is the principle of wu wei:

> The rivers and seas are lords of a hundred valleys. This is because their strength is in lowliness; they are kings of them all. So it is that the perfect master wishing to lead them, he follows. Thus, though he is above them he follows. Thus, though he is above them, men do not feel him to be an injury. And since he will not strive, none strive with him.

The world is full of people who are determined to be somebody or give trouble. They want to get ahead to stand out. Such ambition has no use for a gung fu man, who rejects all forms of self-assertiveness and competition:

> One who tries to stand on tiptoe cannot stand still. One who stretches his legs too far cannot walk. One who advertises himself too much is ignored. One who is too insistent on his own view finds few to agree with him. One who claims too much credit does not get even what he deserves. One who is too proud is soon humiliated. These are condemned as extremes of greediness and self-destructive activity. Therefore, one who acts naturally avoids such extremes.

> Those who know do not speak;
> Those who speak do not know.
> Stop your senses: Let sharp things be blunted,
> Tangles resolved, The light tempered

And turmoil subdued;
For this is mystic unity in which the wise man is moved
Neither by affection,
Nor yet by estrangement
Or profit or loss
Or honor or shame.
Accordingly, by all the world,
He is held highest.

A gung fu man, if he is really good, is not proud at all. Pride is a sense of worth which derives from something that is not organically part of oneself. Pride emphasizes the importance of the superiority of one's status in the eyes of others. There is fear and insecurity in pride because when one aims at being highly esteemed, and having achieved such status, he is automatically involved in the fear of losing his status. Then protection of one's status appears to be his most important need, and this creates anxiety.

The less promise and potency in the self, the more imperative is the need for pride. One is proud when he identifies himself with an imaginary self; the core of pride is self-rejection.

As we know that gung fu is aiming at self-cultivation; and, therefore, the inner self is one's true self; so in order to realize his true self, a gung fu man lives without being dependent upon the opinion of others. Since he is completely self-sufficient he can have no fear of not being esteemed. A gung fu man devotes himself to being self-suffi-

The Tao of Gung Fu

cient, and never depends upon the external rating by others for his happiness. A gung fu master, unlike the beginner, holds himself in reserve, is quiet and unassuming, without the least desire to show off. Under the influence of gung fu training his proficiency becomes spiritual and he himself, grown ever freer through spiritual struggle, is transformed. To him, fame and status mean nothing.

Thus wu wei is the art of artlessness, the principle of no principle. To state it in terms of gung fu, the genuine beginner knows nothing about the way of blocking and striking, and much less of his concern for himself. When an opponent tries to strike him, he instinctively parries it. This is all he can do. But as soon as his training starts, he is taught how to defend and attack, where to keep the mind, and many other technical tricks—which makes his mind stop at various junctures. For this reason whenever he tries to strike the opponent he feels unusually hampered (he has lost altogether the original sense of innocence and freedom). But as months and years go by, as his training acquires fuller maturity, his bodily attitude and his way of managing the technique move toward no-mindednes which resembles the state of mind he had at the very beginning of training when he knew nothing, when he was altogether ignorant of the art. The beginning and the end thus turn into next-door neighbors. On the musical scale, one may start with the lowest pitch and gradually ascend to the highest. When the highest is reached, one finds it is located next to the lowest.

In a similar way, when the highest stage is reached in the study of Taoist teaching, a gung fu man turns into a kind of simpleton who knows nothing of Tao, nothing of its teachings, and is devoid of all learning. Intellectual calculations are lost sight of and a state of no-mindedness prevails. When the ultimate perfection is attained, the body and limbs perform by themselves what is assigned to them to do with no interference from the mind. The technical skill is so automatized it is completely divorced from conscious efforts.

ON EASTERN
AND WESTERN HYGIENE

There is a big difference between the Chinese hygiene and the Western hygiene. Some of the obvious ones are these: Chinese exercises are rhythmic, whereas the Western ones are dynamic and full of tension; the Chinese exercise seeks to merge harmoniously with nature, Western exercise seeks to dominate it; the Chinese exercise is both a way of life and mental cultivation, while the Western exercise is merely a sport or a physical calisthenic.

Perhaps the main difference is the fact that the Chinese hygiene is yin (softness), while the Western hygiene is yang (hardness). We can compare the Western mind with an oak tree that stands firm and rigid against the strong wind. When the wind becomes stronger, the oak tree cracks. The Chinese mind, on the other hand, is like the bamboo that bends with the strong wind. When the wind ceases, that is, when it goes to the extreme and changes, the bamboo springs back stronger than before.

The Tao of Gung Fu

Western hygiene is a gratuitous waste of energy. The over-exertion and overdevelopment of bodily organs involved in Western athletics is detrimental to one's health. Chinese hygiene, on the other hand, throws its emphasis in conservation of energy; the principle is always that of moderation, as opposed to going to extremes. Whatever exercise there may be consists of harmonious movements calculated to normalize but not to excite one's bodily regimen.

It starts out with mental regimen as a basis, of which the sole object is to bring about peace and calmness of mind. With this as the basis, it aims at stimulating a normal functioning of the internal process of respiration and blood circulation.

A MOMENT OF UNDERSTANDING

Gung fu is a special kind of skill; a fine art rather than just a physical exercise. It is a subtle art of matching the essence of the mind to that of the techniques in which it has to work. The principle of gung fu is not a thing that can be learned, like a science, by fact-finding and instruction in facts. It has to grow spontaneously, like a flower, in a mind free from emotions and desires. The core of this principle of gung fu is Tao—the spontaneity of the universe.

After four years of hard training in the art of gung fu, I began to understand and felt the principle of gentleness—the art of neutralizing the effect of the opponent's effort and minimizing the expenditure of one's energy. All these must be done in calmness and without striving. It sounded simple, but in actual application it was difficult. The moment I engaged in combat with an opponent, my mind was completely perturbed and unstable. And after a series of exchanging blows and kicks, all my theory of gentleness was gone. My only thought at this point was "somehow or other I must beat him and win!"

My instructor at the time, Professor Yip Man, head of the Wing Chun school of gung fu, would come up to me and say "Loong, relax and calm your mind. Forget about yourself and follow the opponent's movement. Let your mind, the basic reality, do the counter-movement without any interfering deliberation. Above all, learn the art of detachment."

"That was it!" I thought. "I must relax!" However, right then I had just done something contradictory against my will. That occurred at the precise moment I said "I" $<+>$ "must" $<->$ "relax." The demand for effort in "must" was already inconsistent with the effortlessness in "relax." When my acute self-consciousness grew to what the psychologists refer to as the "double-bind" type, my instructor would again approach me and say "Loong, preserve yourself by following the natural bends of things and don't interfere. Remember never to assert yourself against nature; never be in frontal opposition to any problems, but to control it by swinging with it. Don't practice this week. Go home and think about it."

The following week I stayed home. After spending many hours of meditation and practice, I gave up and went sailing alone in a junk. On the sea I thought of all my past training and got mad at myself and punched the water! Right then—at that moment—a thought suddenly struck me; was not this water the very essence of gung fu? Hadn't this water just now illustrated to me the principle of gung fu? I struck it but it did not suffer hurt. Again I struck it with all of my might—yet it was not wounded! I then tried to grasp a handful of it but this proved impossible. This water, the softest substance in the world and what could be contained in the smallest jar, only

seemed weak. In reality, it could penetrate the hardest substance in the world. That was it! I wanted to be like the nature of water.

Suddenly a bird flew by and cast it's reflection on the water. Right then as I was absorbing myself with the lesson of the water, another mystic sense of hidden meaning revealed itself to me; should not the thoughts and emotions I had when in front of an opponent pass like the reflection of the bird flying over the water? This was exactly what Professor Yip meant by being detached—not being without emotion or feeling, but being one in whom feeling was not sticky or blocked. Therefore in order to control myself I must first accept myself by going with and not against my nature.

I lay on the boat and felt that I had united with Tao; I had become one with nature. I just laid there and let the boat drift freely according to its own will. For at that moment I had achieved a state of inner feeling in which opposition had become mutually cooperative instead of mutually exclusive, in which there was no longer any conflict in my mind. The whole world to me was as one.

The Tao of Gung Fu

CENTERED THOUGHTS—
SOME GUNG FU PRECEPTS

The assimilation of the Tao has its foundation in meekness, tenderness, poverty of spirit, and quietness. These are expressed sometimes by one word, emptiness. An aggressive spirit will be brought low, pride leads to a fall, violence will end in defeat, all which come from misunderstanding the real use of Tao.

Quiescence and nonactivity; not seeking the actual but taking the empty.

In stillness and quietness, without striving or crying; not allowing outside things to entangle one's mind.

Outward change does not move the mind—move forward in harmony with the fluctuating movements of the cosmic spirit.

The yielding will has a reposeful ease, soft as downy feathers; a quietude, a shrinking from action. An appearance of inability to do (the heart is humble, but the work is forceful). Placidity free from anxiety, one acts in harmony with nature; one moves and revolves in the line of creation. One does not move ahead but responds to the fitting influence.

He that humbles himself shall be preserved entire; he that keeps behind shall be put in front; he that bends shall be made straight.

Yielding will overcome anything superior to itself; its strength is boundless.

The highest skill operates on an almost unconscious level.

Who is there that can make muddy water clear? But if allowed to remain still, it will become clear of itself. Who is there that can secure a state of absolute repose? But keep calm and let time go on, and the state of repose will gradually arrest.

Greatness of yielding illustrated by water: Nothing in the world is more yielding and softer than water; yet it penetrates the hardest. Insubstantial, it enters where no room is. It is so fine that it is impossible to grasp a handful of it; strike it, yet it does not suffer hurt; stab it, and it is not wounded.

> If you *try* to remember you will lose.
> Empty your mind, be formless, shapeless. Like water.
> Now you put water into a cup, it becomes the cup.
> You pour water into a bottle, it becomes the bottle.
> You put water into a teapot, it becomes the teapot.
> Now water can flow or creep or drip—or crash!
> Be water, my friend.

> Alive, a man is supple, soft;
> In death, unbending, rigorous.
> All creatures, grass and trees, alive
> are plastic but are pliant too.
> And death, are friable and dry
> Unbending rigor is the mate of death.
> And yielding softness, company of life.

> Unbending soldiers get no victories;
> the stiffest tree is readiest for the ax.
> The strong and mighty belong to the bottom.
> The soft and yielding rise above them all.

To yield is to be preserved whole.
To be bent is to become straight.
To be hollow is to be filled.
To be tattered is to be renewed.

To be in want is to possess.
To have plenty is to be confused.

One should be in harmony with, not rebellion against, the fundamental laws of the universe. This means that we should do nothing that is not natural or spontaneous. The important thing is not to strain in any way. This is best illustrated by the cook, who has used his knife for twenty years and didn't have to replace it. Familiar by long habit with each bone and sinew of the carcass to be cut up, the cook could arrest his sight and other senses and wield the well-tried carving knife with his mind, his method being to work *along* and not *against* the various parts, thus following nature.

Unity of mind and body discards all thoughts of rewards, all hopes of praise and fears of blame, all awareness of one's bodily self, and finally closing the avenues of sense-perception and letting the spirit act as it will.

Emptiness (no mind)

A subtle art of matching the essence of the mind to that of the medium in which it works.

The secret waits for the insight.

Of clouds unclouded by longing; those who are bound by desire see only the outward container.

Tao

Before Confucius, the term *Tao* usually meant a road, or a way of action. Confucius used it as a philosophical concept standing for the right way of action—moral, social, and political. The Taoist used the term *Tao* to stand for the totality of all things, equivalent to what some philosophers have called "the absolute."

The Tao was the basic stuff out of which all things were made. It was simple, formless, desireless, without striving, supremely content.

Endurance is to keep one's place.

Nothing should be consciously planned.

Spontaneous action—of which nature (Tao) was the grand practitioner. This action of nature was real action. The second was action taken with design, premeditated and directed to chosen ends. This, however attractive it might seem, was a forcing of nature and therefore unreal.

That man in whom the truth is bright has no anger.

Be still while you work and keep full control over all.

To know, but to be as though not knowing, is the height of wisdom.

The stillness in stillness is not the real stillness; only when there is stillness in movement does the universal rhythm manifest.

Firmness is concealed in softness; softness in firmness. Activity includes inactivity; each being the cause of the other.

Avoid trials of skill; at first it's all friendliness but in the end it's all antagonism.

To defend is to attack, to attack is to defend.

Firmness cannot be for long, and softness cannot be always in the defensive.

If you feel emptiness, strike in a straight line.

Sparring

In sparring the mind must be quiet and calm; the attention concentrated, and the energy lowered. Besides, straightening the head and body, hollowing the chest, raising the back, lowering the shoulders and elbows, loosening the waist, setting right the sacrum, and keeping the waist, legs, hands, and other parts of the body in perfect harmony are all important. The postures must be natural, capable of stretching and drawing as intended without any awkward strength, and responding immediately after sensing.

Striking

In striking, the momentum of the waist and legs, the motivation and the intrinsic energy must also be added; the hands are employed only as a means to put it through.

Establish nothing in regard to oneself. Let things be what they are, move like water, rest like a mirror, respond like an echo, pass quickly like the nonexistent, and be quiet as purity. Those who gain, lose. Do not precede others, always follow them.

To rest in weakness is strength.

If you would contract, you must first expand. If you would weaken, you must first strengthen. If you would overthrow, you must first raise up. If you would take, you must first give.

The good man wins a victory and then stops; he will not go on to acts of violent winning, he boasteth not, he will not triumph, he shows no arrogance. He wins because he cannot choose. After his victory he will not be overbearing.

The virtue of not striving

The best soldiers are not warlike; the best fighters do not lose their temper. The greatest conquerors are those who overcome their enemies without strife. The greatest directors of men are those who spread peace to the others.

Leave all things to take their natural course, and do not interfere.

Stillness conquers heat.

In the waist, not the limbs, lies the mainspring of the movements of the body. The movements of the limbs are slow and short, while those of the waist are free and long. One turning of a big axis is equivalent to hundreds of turnings of small axes.

Attain complete vacuity, and sedulously preserve a state of repose.

I take softness as my opponent takes firmness, and I take pursuing as he takes retreating.

The pugilism is desirable in activity, and combinable in inactivity. There is no overdoing and no insufficiency; it bends and stretches as intended. It withstands promptly when attacks are quick, and it follows leisurely when attacks are slow. The movements are exact in position, and are invisible at times and visible at others. Too much weight on the left makes the left weak, and too much on the right weakens the right. It is lofty when it rises, and it is deep when it falls. It is far ahead when it advances, and prompt when it retreats. A feather cannot be added, and a fly cannot be placed.

One has ease of mind and absorption in one intention, with neither motives nor presentiments but an outer look of emptiness. Such is the way during practice by yourself.

Give up all thoughts. Set your eyes forward, directed to the spot just in front of the outgoing hand (imagine that an opponent is in front of you). Close your mouth and breathe through your nose. Press your tongue against your palate. Set your shoulders down, lower the elbows, straighten the head, hollow your chest and raise your back in the natural way, loosen the waist with your sacrum right in the middle. Do not force your strength. Raise your spirit and breathe down from the psychic-center (2½ inches under the navel), so that you may feel at ease in every part of your body and the blood may circulate smoothly. The chief movements are done with the waist, rising and lowering alternately like waves. The four limbs and all other parts of the body should correspond with each other, as music with rhythm. The hand movements are composed of two kinds: one of yang (substantiality, firmness, positive, etc.) and one of yin (insubstantiality, softness, negative, etc.). Steps are light and changeable like those of a cat, and also of two classes (yin and yang). Be natural and in the right position while standing and you will be filled with spirit and energy.

You must will to use your energy.

Unperturbed mind.

Be soft yet not yielding; strong yet not hard.

Self-culture—reduction of desire; suppression of the senses—gives power to govern the mind.

To see oneself is to be clear of right. Mighty is he who conquers himself.

Sideways force can be broken though by straight force. Straight force can be stopped by sideways force.

Footwork, hand technique, and body movement; these three ways, if performed right, will floor even a giant.

If there is firmness in softness, you can never break through; if there is no softness in firmness, then it is not strong at all.

When facing an opponent your expression must be like a cat ready to get a mouse.

When he uses strength, I don't use it; when he doesn't use it, I use inner energy. In other words, softness for firmness and firmness for softness.

When you reach a certain point, stop and don't go any further. After bending, stretch. Fit your movement into that of your opponent. Remember every movement should be connected. Although outside seems like it's stopped, inside your energy must not stop, your mind being ahead of your opponent all the time.

In the morning, never face east; at night or rather in the evening, never face west.

Move like a wave, turn like a wheel, slow like an eagle, walk like a cat, fast as lightening, jump up like a monkey, come down like a bird, stand like a tree, stop suddenly like a cock.

The division of gung fu techniques

The gung fu techniques are roughly divided into four ways:

1. Striking of the hand

2. Kicking of the leg

3. The thirty-six throws

4. The seventy-two wrist and arm locks (which also include other parts of holding and choking techniques)

To become one with nature

If I feel in my heart that I am wrong, I must stand in fear even though my opponent is the least formidable of men. But if my own heart tells me that I am right, I shall go forward even against thousands and tens of thousands.

You are required only to perform your own mission—without any thoughts of aggressiveness or competition. Follow the will of nature and coordinate your mind and your act; become one with nature and nature will protect you.

If you would not spill the wine, do not fill the glass too full. If you wish your blade to hold it's edge, do not try to make it over-keen.

Selections from the Tao Te Ching

Rank and arrogance add up to ruin.
The ten thousand things come into being
And I have watched them return.
No matter how luxuriantly they flourish
Each must go back to the root from which it came.
This returning to the root is called quietness;
It is the fulfillment of one's destiny.

That each must fulfill destiny is the eternal pattern.
To know the eternal pattern is to be enlightened.

He who knows it not will be blasted and withered by
misfortune.

He who knows the eternal pattern is all-encompassing; is
completely impartial.

Being impartial, he is kingly;

Being kingly, he is like heaven;

Being like heaven, he is at one with Tao.

Being at one with Tao he is like it, imperishable.

Though his body may disappear into the ocean of existence,

He is beyond all harm.

On tiptoe your stance is unsteady.

Long strides make your progress unsure.

Show off and you get no attention;

Your boasting will mean you have failed.

Asserting yourself brings no credit;

Be proud and you never will lead.

To persons of the Tao, these traits can only bring distrust;

They seem like extra food for parasites.

So those who choose the Way,

Will never give them peace.

Sit and forget; and breathe softly like a little child.

Desire not to desire, and you will not value things difficult
to obtain.

Learning without thought brings ensnarement. Thought
without learning totters.

The heavy is the foundation for the light;

So quietness is master of the deed.

The wise man, though having traveled all the day,

Will not be separated from his goods.

So even if the scene is glorious to view,

He keeps his place, at peace, above it all.

For how can one who rules ten thousand chariots,

Give up to lighter moods, as all the world may do?

If he is trivial,
His ministers are lost;
If he is strenuous,
There is no master then.

Those who know do not talk.
Those who talk do not know.
Stop our senses, close the doors;
Let sharp things be blunted,
Tangles resolved, the light.
Tempered and turmoil subdued;
For this is mystic unity
In which the wise man is moved
Neither by affection nor yet by estrangement
Or profit or loss
Or honor or shame.
Accordingly, by all the world,
He is held highest.

The Tao of Gung Fu

Part 4

IDEAS AND OPINIONS

TRADITIONS AND HISTORIES OF CHINESE GUNG FU

There are innumerable schools of gung fu in both northern and southern parts of China. Among some of the well-known schools are the following:

> pa kua, hsing-i, tang lang, ying jow pai, Tam tui, northern Shaolin, lohan, mizong, hu chuan, cha chuan, hou chuan, Wing Chun, Chow ga, lung ying moshiu, Bak Hok, northern Shaolin, Choy Lay Fut, Hung kuen, Choy ga, Fut ga, Mok ga, Yal Gung Moon, Lee ga, Lao ga, etc.

Some of the styles

Choy Lay Fut gung fu

Choy Lay Fut was founded by Chan Heung in Kwangtung Province. Like many of the southern Chinese youths, he was first introduced to the popular southern Shaolin style of Hung kuen by his uncle. Later on, he trained with a Lay (or Lee) Yau Saan. Still yearning for more knowledge, he went to Mt. Law Fow and sought out the Monk Choy Fook. Before long, Chan Heung was to combine all his learning to form his own style, and named it the Choy Lay Fut style. To honor his previous instructors, he named his style after them. Choy was named after Mon Choy Fook, Lay, after Lay Yau Saan, and finally, because Hung kuen is one of the many branches of the Shaolin Buddhist Temple, the term Fut (Buddhist) is adopted.

Choy Lay Fut is essentially a long-range style of boxing, relying on a strong "horse" [stance], and known for its joint-locking techniques, the backfist, the downward swing, and the knuckle fist. There are many empty-hand sets (forms) in this southern style: the long-range fist, Buddhist fist, t'ai, ping, teen gok fists, etc. In weapon sets there are baat gwa lance, willow leaf, double swords, eighteen staff, etc. Among the more famous practitioners of this style were Chang Hung Sing, the leading disciple of the founder Chan Heung. Presently, many of the Choy Lay Fut training halls are also known as Hung Sing Kwoon (Kwoon = training hall). Chang's own leading disciple, by the name of Chan Sing, was quite a popular Chinese boxing instructor in Fut Saan of Southern China. Tam Saam was another able Choy Lay Fut practitioner.

Iron forearm gung fu

According to the teachers of this system, it is very easy to master. Simply find a pole or column and begin hitting it with your forearm very lightly. Do this every day, hitting it with all parts of your forearm—front, back, and sides. Gradually, increase your striking force.

銕臂膊圖式

Eventually you should venture outside and find a tree to practice on. This tree should have lumpy bark on it. Do this for one year. After one year, you should look to train on very smooth rocks. Continue practicing on the rocks until you can break them with your forearm. When you can do this, your forearm will be as strong as iron.

Paper tent gung fu

This kind of gung fu is totally concentrated on the fist. Although considered a hard style of gung fu, if you understand its essence, then you will realize that it is not only a hard style of gung fu, but rather an interchanging of the hard and soft method. In the beginning of the practice, you should use waste paper and thin string. Tie it up into a bundle so that it looks like a small bamboo suitcase or picnic basket. The width and length should be a twenty-inch cube. The two sides should be slightly longer (more rectangular in shape). In the center fasten a long string to be used as a retriever. This item is called "the paper tent." Place the paper tent on top of a long table. This table should measure about nine feet in length by two feet. The trainee should be at one end of the table, sitting in the a semi-squatting position or "bowl horse" stance. With your left hand pulling on the string, make a fist with your right hand and aggressively strike the paper tent. Strike out with your fist. In the beginning, the paper tent will barely move, but later on it will be jumping outward. After you strike with your fist, you should use your left hand to hold the string and strike the tent with your right hand. Continue on with this punch and pull motion until you are tired out, or until the left and right hand have lost their ability to act in a coordinated fashion.

Start out using waste paper (it should weigh more than 20 Chinese ounces). Then, as you progress, wrap some lead weights inside until, over time, it weighs over 100 ounces. As the weight of the paper tent increases, so should the punching repetitions and, when you've reached the point where it feels like there is no resistance—even with the weight inside—and your coordination does not falter so that you can return the punch with each pull—then you are more than halfway to achieving success in this type of gung fu. The strength of the punching fist will be amazingly increased by this method, but this should by no means be viewed as the peak of accomplishment. What you should do at this point is to remove slabs or leaves out of the center of the table, so that the paper tent now has to travel over a large whole without falling through to the floor. At first, you won't be able to return it back and forth so easily, but several months later, you will achieve the desired effect of popping it back and forth without it falling through to the floor. At this point, remove another leaf or section from the table and continue on with your practice. Eventually, you should be able to remove all of the sections from the table until you only have one-third of the original length of the table remaining. At this point the paper tent should follow the fist strikes and you should be able to make it travel aerodynamically back and forth without it dropping through. At this point you will have mastered this exercise and can now move on to trying your skill against people. You should be able to drive your opponent back over ten Chinese yards—or more! And if I were to face multiple opponents in a fight, I would employ this method of attack because it is the easiest winning move. This type of gung fu is right in the middle of yin/yang as it contains elements of yin, which is why it is so effective. It's funny that this paper tent hand movement definitely has just the right balance of the hard and soft complementing each other.

紙篷功圖式

Chinese weapons

Gung fu includes techniques of hands, feet, knees, elbows, shoulders, head, and thighs; the thirty-six throws; the seventy-two joint locks, and the eighteen different weapons. Swordplay is the most difficult of all arts in gung fu. It requires at least ten years of hard training to be a master of it. The sword must be united with the mind, and be used as the limb of the body.

鏜 矛 戟 槌

單刀式
Single Oar

三節棍
Three section chain
stick (staff)

蹬腿后扎槍
Spearplay

雙刀式
Two swordplay

上步肩背棍
Stick play
(staff)

騰空提膝下截刀

大刀對棍
Big Sword against Stick

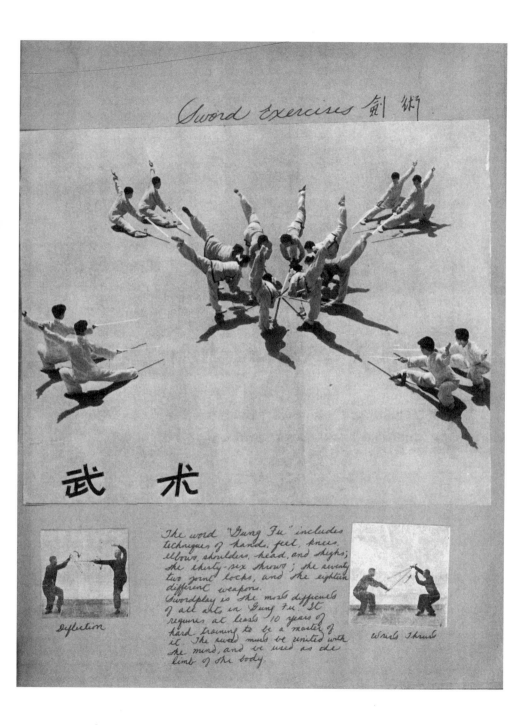

Sword exercises 劍術

武 术

Deflection

The word "Gung Fu" includes techniques of hands, feet, knees, elbows, shoulders, head, and thighs; the thirty-six throws; the seventy two joint locks, and the eighteen different weapons.

Swordplay is the most difficult of all arts in Gung Fu. It requires at least 10 years of hard training to be a master of it. The sword must be united with the mind, and be used as the limb of the body.

Wrist Thrust

Masters of gung fu and their legends

Master Kuo Yu Cheung

Master Kuo is from Kwong Sho State, and is noted for his spear play and his so-called iron palms. Legend had it that he had once killed a horse with a slight twist of his palm, and when they examined the dead horse later, they couldn't find any bruise outside; but inside the horse, the internal organs were all smashed. Master Kuo also broke twelve bricks with a slap of his palm. Master Kuo is adept in both of the soft (internal) and firm (external) schools of gung fu. The above demonstration was an example of the intermediate technique of the soft school. Here the internal (yin) energy is used. Master Kuo's instructor, Professor Shin, could break and split one hundred pieces of tissue papers in a similar way.

Professor Shin Look Ton (Master of the Three Soft Schools)

Professor Shin started gung fu when he was only a child and devoted himself to the art till he died at the age of ninety-three. He had taught millions of students and is noted for his techniques all over China.

Professor Kim Kai Fook (Master of the Sil Lum School)

Professor Kim was another great master of gung fu who had practiced the art throughout his whole life. Many noted experts of the various schools had come to study under Professor Kim. He was noted for his speed, his internal power, and his famous puncture heart kick. At the age of eighty, he could beat any instructors living around that area.

Master Law Kon Yuk (Leader of the Praying Mantis School)

Master Law, a giant who moved like lightening, was born in Shan Tung Province. He was adept in all the arts of his school, including sword, spear, club, etc. He was the head instructor of the Mantis Clan in the famous Jing Mo gung fu Institute of northern China.

Professor Ng Kam Chuen
(Leader of the Ng Tai Kik School)

Famous in both northern and southern China, Professor Ng had taught thousands and thousands of students. In his time, none dared to try out with him. His son, Ng Koon Yee, succeeded him as the present head of the school.

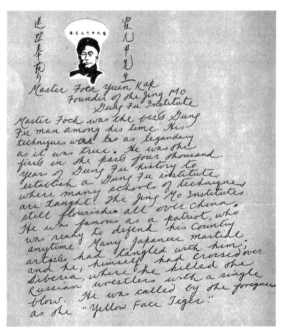

Master Fock Yuen Kap
(Founder of the Jing Mo gung fu Institute)

Master Fock was the best gung fu man of his time. His technique was as legendary as it was true. He was the first in the past four thousand years of gung fu history to establish a gung fu institute where many schools of techniques were taught. The Jing Mo Institutes still flourish all over China. He was famous as a patriot, ready to defend his country anytime. Many Japanese martial artists had tangled with him, and he, himself, had crossed over Siberia where he killed the Russian wrestlers with a single blow. He was called by the foreigners the "Yellow-Faced Tiger."

Professor Yip Man
(Leader of the Wing Chun School)

The last Master of the Wing Chun school is Professor Yip, born in Fut San in Southern China. Professor Yip started a study of the various schools of gung fu at the age of eight, until he met Professor Chan Wa Shun and immediately devoted his full energies to his art, the Wing Chun school. Now he is the present leader of that school. Professor Yip is truly a gung fu great, and is respected by other instructors of various schools. He is famous for his "sticking hands," in which he attaches his hands to the opponent and subdues him with his eyes shut! Even at the age of sixty he was still active, and none of his students could touch him.

Professor Yang Kin Hou (Leader of the Famous "Yang School" of t'ai kik)

Professor Yang, son of the late Yang Lo Sim, champion of Peking, was a gung fu great. He was known as a formidable opponent by other schools' instructors, and with a bamboo stick he could disable any armed opponent. He could also place a bird on his palm, and the bird could not fly away. This feat proved his sensitivity of feeling in the direction of strength. For as soon as the bird was ready to spring and fly away from his open palm, he just simply dropped his palm slightly. Professor Yang died in 1917.

Professor Yang Jing Po

Master Yang was the second son of Professor Yang Kin Hou. His technique was also very fine. Outside he looked gentle and soft, but inside was firm as a rock. He left three sons; the eldest is Yang Shou Chung who is heading the Kin Mun Tai Kik School in Hong Kong.

A DISCUSSION ON CHINESE GUNG FU

(with Bruce Lee, James Y. Lee, and Leo Fong)

QUESTION: First of all, what is the difference between the *internal* school and the *external* school of gung fu? The so-called soft and hard styles?.

BRUCE LEE: The difference, like any other martial art, is in their approach; as to the separation of so-called external and internal, or hard and soft, it is an illusion. You see, in reality, gentleness/firmness is one inseparable force of one unceasing interplay of movement. Take a person riding a bicycle: if he wishes to go somewhere, he cannot pump on both pedals at the same time or not pump on them at all. In order to move forward he has to pump on one pedal and release the other. So the motion of going forward requires this "oneness" of pumping and releasing. Pumping, then, is the result of releasing and vice versa, each being the cause and result of the other. Of course we hear a lot of the teachers claiming their styles are soft and others are hard; these people are clinging blindly to one partial view of the totality. Because if they have understood and transcended the real meaning of gentleness and firmness, they wouldn't have made such an impossible separation. I was asked by a so-called gung fu master once—one of those that really looked the part, with beard and all—as to what I think of yin (soft) and yang (firm). I simply answered "baloney!" Of course, he was quite shocked at my answer and still has not come to the realization that "it" is never two.

So we must realize, then, that it is not a matter of the soft versus the firm, because, as I've pointed out, that gentleness and firmness are always as a whole and are equally important as well as unavoidably interdependent on each other. If one rejects either the firm or the soft, this will lead to separation, and separation will run to extremes. Those who cling to either extreme are known as either physically bound or intellectually bound, though the former are more bearable. At least the physically bound do struggle.

QUESTION: There seems to be a lot more styles or schools in gung fu than in karate. Could you tell us how many—and the basic differences between them?

BRUCE LEE: That is a difficult question because there are so many different styles; however, let me put it this way. Fundamentally, all styles claim that their method is able to cope with "all" types of attacks. That means each and every style is complete and total. In other words, their structure covers all possible lines and angles, as well as being capable of retaliating from all angles and lines. Now, since all possible lines and angles are covered, where come all the "different" styles? Take Western boxing: disregard whether the boxer assumes a crouch stance or an upright stance, hands held high or low, he still uses the basic tools of the jab, hook, cross, uppercut. They do not have fancy terms for those who crouch as the "turtle style" or for those who stand upright as the "giraffe style." And do not let anyone tell you that martial art is different from boxing. True that they do not use kicks or elbows, but basically and ultimately all arts return to the same truth. I guess he who claims his style is really different from the others must assume his stance on his head, and when he strikes he must turn and spin three times before doing so. After all, how many ways are there to come in on an opponent without deviating from the natural and direct path? By "different" probably these instructors go only for straight lines, or maybe just round lines, or maybe only kicking, or maybe even just "looking different;" flapping here and flicking there. To me, styles that cling to one partial aspect of combat are actually in bondage. You see, a choice method, however exacting, fixes its practitioners in an enclosed pattern. I always say that actual combat is never fixed, has no boundaries or limits, and is constantly changing from moment to moment. Because one does not want to be made uncertain and be engaged in broken rhythm, so he establishes a fixed pattern of combat, a cooperative pattern of rhythmic relationship with his partner. As his margin of freedom is getting narrower and narrower, he becomes a slave to the pattern and accepts the pattern to be the real thing. Such exclusive drilling on a set pattern of one's choice will only lead its practitioners to clogginess, because basically it is a practice of resistance. In reality, the way of combat is never based on personal choice and fancies, and one will soon find out that his choice routines lack pliability and are incapable of adapting to the ever-changing swift movement of combat. All of a sudden his opponent is alive and no longer a cooperative robot. In other words, once conditioned in a partialized style, its practitioner faces his opponent through a screen of resistance. In reality, he is merely performing his stylized blocks and listening to his own screams.

QUESTION: I understand from you that there are more phonies in gung fu than there are in other arts. What is your advice to the general public that would like to take up the art?

BRUCE LEE: Mr. James Y. Lee and Mr. Leo Fong here both have gone through the experience and I think it will be interesting to listen to them. Both have spent quite a long time on the Chinese art and Mr. Fong is also a ni-dan [second-degree black belt, in tae kwon do] in Korean karate.

JAMES LEE: It is a sad fact that there is an alarming rate of self-styled "masters" in the Chinese arts. One of the most common traits of the phonies are the mysterious types, or the so-called hidden power types who strive to convince the students that, while their regular program is just plain or ordinary in appearance, once the student is accepted, then—and only then—will their hidden powers be revealed. Anyway, the masters of this type try to create an atmosphere of mysticism and humbleness. To them this humility and mysticism serves to get the idea across of being a master disguised in meekness. Of course, as always, these masters are never seen in free-style sparring—"sparring is too dangerous" or "we are not unsophisticated street fighters," etc. In fact, if their students sit down and think, they quickly realize that they have never really seen their masters do anything convincing along the lines of actual combat. In other words, the "hidden power" is just that, always hidden away!

LEO FONG: Then there are those types better known as the "chop suey" masters. These masters know practically all the forms and sets of the so-called northern and southern styles, internal and external systems, of course, including all the weapon sets. In fact, once there is a new gung fu book published either in Hong Kong, Formosa [Taiwan], or Red China, and if they can get a hand on it, it will be included in their systems. Some of these masters are so brilliant, they can mix the movements all up with five or six different forms. Of course, all forms and no freestyle sparring.

JAMES LEE: Talking about freestyle sparring, this activity seems to be lacking with most of the self-styled phonies. Mr. Bruce Lee aptly put it this way; he says "When a runner gives a demonstration, he runs. When a swimmer gives a demonstration, he swims. When a boxer gives a demonstration, he spars. Now when a "professor" or "master" gives a demonstration, he . . . ?" Well, anyway, the next group is the gimmick performers. Since they will never spar, they have to substitute the real thing with some circus acts and show the audience their internal power by breaking things or have things broken on their bodies.

BRUCE LEE: Many of these self-styled masters who have been preaching their doctrines for many years have gained some surface knowledge and some established sales pitch. This is quite unfortunate for those who are already confused but sincere in wanting to learn gung fu. This includes black belters from various martial art systems. You see, most of these confused souls are seeking for something higher, something more complex. So they begin to learn more advanced forms that are "different" (efficiency is no longer a concern here) from what they have seen. The end is efficiency in broken rhythm sparring, but the means—the way-out forms—are being drilled upon every day. As the forms become less and less real, the practitioners drift further and further away from the end—the reality of martial art. Finally, all their efforts will have to concentrate on the means and the end is forgotten. Not only that, but an unrelated standard of judgment is established within the systems, like "the horse stance is not firm and flat," or "the energy is not applied correctly," etc. In short, even though one might get knocked down and out, when he comes to, he will probably say something like "Yeah, but he was off-balance when he hit me, his heel was up, his hand was not on the hip, etc., etc., etc. Really, if one approaches these "professors" with common sense, he is seldom wrong. In other words, one should evaluate an instructor as to his basic requirements in an all-out combat, and not on his showing him a form or a movement or two. Ranks, if they have them, are not important as compared to his actual ability, nor is looking beautiful as compared to his efficiency. Really, if one is efficient, his form will be a delight, but a beautiful form does not make an efficient fighter.

QUESTION: We have seen a lot of demonstrations wherein the demonstrator allows people to push him on the arm and they cannot move him or to have people punch him on the stomach. What is your comment on this?

BRUCE LEE: This is really strange. I mean, you will never see a Western boxer demonstrate what you have just said. You see, a Western boxer is primarily a fighter and, when he demonstrates, he spars. Anyway, first of all, in a fight, an attacker will throw punches and kicks at you, he won't push you. Also, why spend years of training on the stomach to be able to take a full-force punch in that region—only to be blinded by a mere finger jab? True, stomach exercises are vital, but does a strong stomach mean a good martial artist? I hope the practitioners

will concentrate on the essentials instead of fooling around with gimmicks. The essentials are broken rhythm, sparring, and efficient techniques.

Note: James Y. Lee was a close friend and student of Bruce Lee from 1959 until his death in December of 1972. He and Bruce had a school in Oakland in 1964, which James continued to operate after Bruce had gone to Los Angeles. James had an extensive background in martial art before he met Bruce, but upon their meeting he became an avid follower of Bruce's.

Leo Fong is a practitioner of gung fu from Sacramento, California, and was at times a student of Bruce's.

THE QUESTION OF PSYCHIC CENTER

Different schools of gung fu instructors teach their students to keep their mind in the psychic center (dan t'ien); located two-and-a-half or sometimes one-and-a-half inches below the navel. The method is to breathe deeply down to this lower region of the abdomen; this will enable you to lower the center of gravity and be fast in shifting from one position to another. It is also believed that tremendous psychic power will be generated from such practice. This is fine for the beginner, but to the gung fu master (also the Taoist or Zen masters), what is highest is nothingness.

The mind (if there is such a thing) should pervade and fill up the whole body and flow freely throughout. The so-called mind should be all-embracing; it is here and there and everywhere. If you imprison your mind in the lower abdomen, every other part of the body will feel its absence. What is more is the fact that if you can localize the mind in the lower abdomen, when you have to use it extra time and energy are wasted in trying to maneuver the mind from this lower abdomen to the needed part. The gung fu master believes in a unity in multiplicity and a wholeness of parts. What I recommend is to forget about this partiality of localizing the mind to anywhere. In fact, forget about the mind; when you have no concern of the mind, it will start to open up and become ready to respond freely to any situation. It can do this because the mind is not attached or confined (a state of wu-hsin).

When the mind is not confined anywhere, it is everywhere. Did you know that a centipede was walking along nicely when another bug stopped him to find out how he managed to walk with hundreds of legs? Well, the centipede stopped and began to consciously describe the process of his walking. And do you know what happened? The centipede fell flat on his face.

MY VIEW ON GUNG FU

Some instructors of martial art favor forms, the more complex and fancy the better. Some, on the other hand, are obsessed with super mental power (like Captain Marvel or Superman). Still some favor deformed hands and legs, and devote their time to fighting bricks, stones, boards, etc.

To me, the extraordinary aspect of gung fu lies in its simplicity. Gung fu is simply the direct expression of one's feeling with the minimum of movements and energy. Every movement is being so of itself without the artificialities with which people tend to complicate it. The easy way is always the right way, and gung fu is nothing at all special; the closer to the true way of gung fu, the less wastage of expression there is.

Instead of facing combat in its suchness, quite a few systems of martial art accumulate "fanciness" that distorts and cramps their practitioners and distracts them from the actual reality of combat, which is simple and direct and nonclassical. Instead of going immediately to the heart of things, flowery forms and artificial techniques (organized despair!) are ritually practiced to simulate actual combat. Thus, instead of *being* in combat, these practitioners are idealistically *doing* something about combat.

Worse still, "super mental this" and "spiritual that" are ignorantly incorporated until these practitioners are drifting so much further and further into the distance of abstraction and mystery that what they're doing resembles anything (from acrobatics to modern dancing) but the actual reality of combat.

All these complexities are actually futile attempts to arrest and fix the ever-changing movements in combat and to dissect and analyze them like a corpse. Real combat is not fixed and is very much alive. Such means of practice (a form of paralysis) will only solidify and condition what was once fluid and alive. When you get off sophistication and whatnot, and look at it realistically, these robots (practitioners, that is) are blindly devoted to the systematic uselessness of practicing routines or stunts that lead nowhere.

Gung fu is to be looked at without fancy suits and matching ties, and it will remain a secret when we anxiously look for sophistication and "deadly" techniques. If there are really any secrets at all, they must have been missed by the seeking and striving of its practitioners (after all, how many ways are there to come in on an opponent without deviating too much from the natural course?). True gung fu values the wonder of the ordinary, and the cultivation of gung fu is not daily increase, but daily decrease. Being wise in gung fu does not mean adding more, but to be able to get off with ornamentation and be simply simple—like a sculptor building a statue, not by adding but by hacking away the unessential so that the truth will be revealed unobstructed. In short, gung fu is satisfied with one's bare hand without the fancy decoration of colorful gloves which tend to hinder the natural function of the hand.

Art is the expression of the self. The more complicated and restrictive a method is, the lesser the opportunity for the expression of one's original sense of freedom! The techniques, though they play an important role in the early stage, should not be too restrictive, complex, or mechanical. If we cling to them we will become bound by their limitations. Remember, you are *expressing* the technique and not *doing* the technique. When someone attacks you it is not technique number one (or is it technique number two, stance two, section four?) that you are doing, but the moment you become aware of his attack you simply move in like sound and echo without any deliberation. It is as though when I call you, you answer me or when I throw something to you, you catch it, that's all.

WHAT IT ALL ADDS UP TO

Before I studied the art, a punch to me is just like a punch, a kick just like a kick. After I've studied the art, a punch is no longer a punch, a kick no longer a kick. Now that I've understood the art, a punch is just like a punch, a kick just like a kick.

There is nothing much in this art. Take things as they are. Punch when you have to punch. Kick when you have to kick.

Not being tense but ready, not thinking but not dreaming, not being set but flexible—It is being wholly and quietly alive, aware and alert, ready for whatever may come.

The height of cultivation runs to simplicity. Halfway cultivation leads to ornamentation.

It's not daily increase but daily decrease—hack away the unessential!

Would that we could at once strike with the eyes! In the long way from the eye through the arm to the fist, how much [time] is lost!

Please do not disregard your five natural senses to rely on a so-called sixth!

I'm moving and not moving at all. I'm like the moon's reflection upon the waves that ever goes on rolling and rocking.

Give up thinking as though not giving it up. Observe the techniques as though not observing.

To change with change is the changeless state.

The stillness in stillness is not the real stillness, only when there is stillness in movement does the universal rhythm manifest.

Nothingness cannot be confined; the softest thing cannot be snapped.

QUESTIONS AND ANSWERS

Name 姓名 *LINDA EMERY*

Address 地址 *2332 11TH E.*

Signature *Linda Emery*

(President)

No. 0008

PERMANENT
MEMBER
RANK

1	5
2	6
3	7
4	8

Advice to women

QUESTION: What advice would you give to a woman who is forced to defend herself against a big, powerful brute?

BRUCE LEE: The trouble is that circumstances must dictate what you do. But too many people are looking at what *is* from a position of thinking what *should be*. However, I don't care what you've heard, there's no such thing as a 90-pound weakling tossing a 250-pound giant. And if a 90-pound woman is attacked, the only thing she can do is strike hard at one of three places—the eyeballs, the groin, or the shins. This would be sufficient self-defense to put the man off balance for just a moment. And then she'd better run like hell.

More on definitions

QUESTION: You have mentioned that gung fu goes by many different names. Can you list some of them and also give a definition of gung fu that is common to all styles?

BRUCE LEE: Gung fu, the prevalent term now used in the United States, has quite a few other names. In China, Formosa, and Hong Kong, gung fu is called kuo shu or kuo chi; while in Japan, it is known as kempo. Historically, the name of chuen yung was first found in *The Book of Poetry* and the following chart will show that in different dynasties, gung fu took on a different term.

Chuen yung—*The Book of Poetry*	Chi yung—Ming Dynasty
Wu ni—Chun Chiu Era	Chi ni—Ming Dynasty
Chi chi—Chan Kuo Era	Pai shou—Ching Dynasty
Chi chiao—Han Dynasty	Wu shu—Chinese Republic
Shou po—Han Dynasty	Kuo shu—Chinese Republic
Kung shou—Ni Dynasty	Kuo chi—Chinese Republic

The two words *gung fu* mean accumulation of work or training. However, in the sense of martial art, it means training and discipline toward the *Tao* of an object—be it the Tao of health promotion, the Tao of cultivation of mind, or the Tao of self-protection.

The "best" way to learn

QUESTION: What is the best way for a person to learn Chinese gung fu?

BRUCE LEE: By being himself. The main thing is teaching a man to do his thing, to just be himself. The individual is more important than the style. If a person is awkward, he should not try to be agile. I'm against trying to impose a style on a man. This is an art, an expression of a man's own self.

Do we need more than basics?

QUESTION: I am training with a Chinese instructor who drills us again and again on basics—like side kicks, straight punching, etc. When we spar, we are instructed to use only his chosen basic techniques, though sometimes we can use combinations and everything. Do you not think we need variety?

BRUCE LEE: The best techniques are the simple ones done correctly. And in martial art, it is not how much you have learned, but how much you have absorbed in what you have learned. As long as the basics are on meaningful means that will lead to the ultimate end of actual application in broken rhythm, they are never wasted. Efficient basics are like the strong foundation of a house. Of course, one must avoid basics that have the "aliveness" taken out of them and are "performed" in rhythmic routines. Have patience, my friend. I'm sure your teacher knows what he is doing.

On the need for belts in the martial arts

QUESTION: Most proficient karate people have black belts. Some really advanced masters have red belts. You've been called a master of martial art, so what color belt do you have?

BRUCE LEE: I don't have any belt whatsoever. That is just a certificate. Unless you can really do it—that is, defend yourself successfully in a fight—that belt doesn't mean anything. I think it might be useful to hold your pants up, but that's about it.

The problem with black belts

QUESTION: You seem down on the whole idea of black-belt rankings. Why is this?

BRUCE LEE: There simply isn't time in a man's life—if he were to train the proper oriental way—to receive such an honor. If Orientals can't earn it, surely Americans who practice one or two nights a week can't. I'm very much against this "become a holy terror in three easy lessons" mentality.

The natural versus the supernatural

QUESTION: Some martial artists indicate the "true masters" of their various styles have developed an "inner" spiritual type of gung fu that enables them to perform incredible, almost supernatural feats such as being impervious to swords and knives. Do you think that this kind of thing is real?

BRUCE LEE: I think to be a really good martial artist one already has many things to learn in this life, so why should a person learn that? Therefore, I really don't have any interest in this "supernatural" gung fu. If you ask me what I will do in heaven, I will say this: "There are many things in this life I have not finished. Why should I think about something so far away?" Moreover, I think that those who trust in this "spirit-possessed" power have a vested interest in doing so. Why else would they trust in something so unscientific? I do not think, for example, that a man will not hurt himself when he falls from the twelfth floor of a building—regardless of how proficient he may be in his particular style of gung fu. I also do not believe that a man's flesh is impervious to swords and knives.

The nature of water

QUESTION: Could you please explain the principle of the Glass of Water as it applies to gung fu?

BRUCE LEE: Well, one of the best examples of gung fu is a glass of water. Why? Because it is capable of adapting itself to any situation. If you pour it into a cup, it becomes the cup; if you pour it into a bottle, it becomes the bottle; if you pour it into a glass, it becomes the glass. Water is the softest substance in the world, yet it can penetrate the hardest rock. Water is also insubstantial; by that I mean, you cannot grasp hold of it, you cannot punch it and hurt it. So every gung fu man is trying to do that; to be soft like water, to be flexible and able to adapt himself to the opponent.

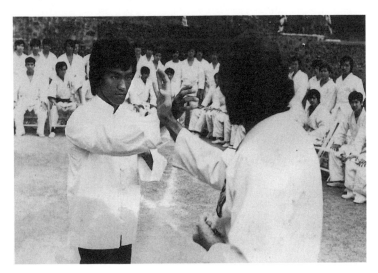

Gung fu versus jujitsu

QUESTION: What is the difference between jujitsu, which seems to be rather long and involved, and gung fu, which is very quick, if you have an opponent?

BRUCE LEE: Sometimes you will read in a book or in a martial arts magazine, that when somebody grabs you, you are told to "first do this, and then this, and then, and then, and then, and then"— thousands of steps before you do a single thing. Of course, these kinds of magazines would teach you to be "feared by your enemies and admired by your friends" and everything else in between. But in gung fu, it always involves a very fast motion. For instance, if a guy grabs your hand, it's not the idea in gung fu to do so many steps.

The Tao of Gung Fu

Rather you should simply stomp your opponent right on the instep—he'll let go. This is what we mean by "simplicity." The same thing applies in striking; it has to be based on a very minimum motion so that everything can be directly expressed in one motion—boom!—and he's gone. Doing it gracefully.

More on wu wei

QUESTION: Why is wu-wei so important in the process of becoming a better martial artist?

BRUCE LEE: The principle of wu-wei is entirely an action of creative intuition, which opens the wellsprings within man. While the action of assertion, man's common tendency, is preconceptual and rational, it cannot penetrate the hidden recesses of creativity. The action of assertion is viewed from the externals of intellection, while the action of nonassertion is activated by the inner light. The former action is limited and finite, the latter free and limitless.

Wu wei and chi sao

QUESTION: I'm still not sure how wu wei ties into the practice of chi sao or sticking hands. Can you explain?

BRUCE LEE: The understanding of chi sao is an inner experience in which the distinction between self and opponent vanishes. It is an intuitive, immediate awareness rather than a mediated, inferential, or intellectual process.

The rise of gung fu

QUESTION: Why do you think that gung fu is becoming so popular these days?

BRUCE LEE: The art of gung fu is gaining popularity, especially among the college students, for it is not merely some fighting tricks or brick-breaking stunts, but it is a philosophical art of self-defense that has 4,000 years of refinement in it. Also, its theory is logical and its application is practical. In addition, gung fu serves to cultivate the mind, to promote health, and to provide a most efficient means of self-protection against any attacks. Additionally, gung fu is comparatively nonstrenuous, and serves to normalize instead of overdeveloping or overexerting the body. However, above all else, gung fu develops confidence, humility, coordination, adaptability, and respect toward others.

The basic theory behind gung fu

QUESTION: What is the basic theory behind gung fu?

BRUCE LEE: Well, the basic idea is simply to "fit" harmoniously into your opponent's movement like the immediacy of the shadow adjusting itself to the moving body. Instead of opposition, there is co-operation. It is like a pliable reed that neither opposes nor gives way in the wind. Every movement in gung fu has a flowing continuity without any dislocation. Defense is attack, attack is defense, each being the cause and result of the other. Its techniques are smooth, short, and extremely fast; they are direct, to the point, and are stripped down to their essential purposes without any wasted motions. Simplicity is the key word in this art—to do the utmost in the minimum of motion and energy. The method of gung fu parallels that of the flow of water, as running water never grows stale.

Applying the centerline and body weight theories to judo

QUESTION: I'm quite taken with your theories regarding the centerline and also putting all of your body weight into your strikes instead of simply arm power. However, I'm a *judoka*—not a gung fu man—and we use throws rather than strikes. Does this render these principles invalid?

BRUCE LEE: Not at all. It is most interesting to work on the coordination of arm and body for that will make a judoka able to exert twice (perhaps triple) his power and a gung fu man to strike his body weight. Using arm force alone is indeed characteristic of the untrained person (in fact, a lot of instructors are practitioners of this) and since striking is mainly used in gung fu, I'll discuss the relationship of arm power and body power (waist or hip movement) in a punch. I'm sure that there will be a similar basic source as in throwing. It will facilitate the analysis of putting in the waist with the arm by dividing the human body into two halves with an imaginary centerline as in Figure one.* Figure two* shows a person releasing his right side and propelling his body weight (as in an ordinary right-hand punch) by bracing himself on his left foot that acts as the hinge around which his right side body weight and power rotates. The hip and shoulder are driven first to the imaginary centerline then the arm comes into play "explosively." The whole idea is to transfer the weight to the opponent's target area before the weight transfers to the left leg. That is also why in stepping in to strike, the leading foot should not land first, or the body weight will rest upon the floor instead of being behind the striking hand. Of course, all these are coordinated very, very fast, but the waist reverse does come a split

*Figures one and two are found on page 41.

second faster. If you manipulate this imaginary centerline it might evolve some new angle for your judo analysis.

From this centerline I was able to construct a nucleus and later on able to jump away from the nucleus and establish out-of-line and broken-rhythm counterattack. By the way, emphasis must be made to the students to throw with their body because of the fact that in terms of force and power, the arms have but one quarter of the force of the body when set in motion. Secondly, the movements of the waist are long and free while those of the arms are short. You can say that one turning of a large axis is equivalent to many turnings of a small axis. The arms exert maximum strength toward the end of the movement—therefore, the arms are the vehicle of force that is released by the body through this centerline idea. Boxing also makes use of this centerline business but expresses it in too big a motion. It is all right at first but later on it should be guided by the principle of simplicity—to express the utmost in the minimum of movements and energy. However, in terms of judo, the movements can be a little larger than in gung fu because judo doesn't involve striking and counter-striking. If I were to work on judo I'd make use of this centerline (I haven't really worked on it—on top of that I have limited knowledge of the subject) and classify the attacks in judo something like:

1. Direct attack—quick and powerful, one action drives in to throw opponent.

2. Combination attack—to combine two or three throws in a row to disturb the opponent's rhythm.

3. Indirect attack—to use false attack to draw a reaction from the opponent and make use of this reaction for your throw— seems like this field is rarely used in oriental systems. Everything starts from immobile to mobile. Feints and what not, if done in a threatening manner, can disturb even a calm and cool operator.

4. Attack by drawing—apparent opening to opponent and counter his attack to it.

There are more than that I'm sure, but in order to build on it, one has to jump out from the classical rigidity and see the field in a more practical light—as weight training (not bodybuilding) has contributed to judo.

IN CONCLUSION

In conclusion I sincerely give this advice to all readers who are about to take up martial art—believe only half of what you see and definitely nothing that you hear. Before you take any lessons from any instructor, find out clearly from him what his method is and request him politely to demonstrate to you how some techniques operate. Use your common sense and if he convinces you, then by all means go ahead.

How does one judge if an instructor is good? Rather, this question should be rephrased to how can one judge if a method or system is good. After all, one cannot learn the speed or power of an instructor, but rather his skill. Thus, the soundness of the system, and not the instructor, is to be considered; the instructor is merely there to point the way and lead his disciples to an awareness that he himself is the one and only one to give true feeling and expression to the system. The system should not be mechanical and complicated but simply simple, with no "magical power." The method (which is ultimately no method) is there to remind one when he has done enough. The techniques have no magical power and are nothing special; they are merely the simplicity of profound common sense.

Do not, however, be impressed by instructors who have brick-breaking hands, invincible stomachs, iron forearms, or even speed for that matter. Remember you cannot learn his ability, but his skill. At any rate, ability to break stones, to take a punch on the body, to jump so many feet off the ground, are but stunts in the Chinese art of gung fu. Of primary importance are the techniques. Breaking a brick and

The Tao of Gung Fu

punching a human being are two different things: a brick does not give, whereas when being hit, a human being spins, falls, etc., thus dissolving the power of the blow. What is the use if one has no technique to bring home his so-called killing stroke? On top of that, bricks and stones do not move and fight back. Thus, the system should be the thing considered and, as mentioned before, a system should not be mechanical, intricate, and fanciful, but simply simple.

What if the "master" does not wish to show you his style? What if he is "too humble" and firmly guards his "deadly" secret? One thing I hope the readers should realize regarding oriental humility and secrecy is that although it is true that highly qualified teachers do not boast and sometimes do not teach gung fu to just anybody, the fact remains that they are only human beings and certainly they have not spent ten, twenty, or thirty years on an art in order to say nothing about it. Even Lao-tzu, the author of the *Tao Te Ching*, and the man who wrote "He who knows does not speak. He who speaks, does not know," wrote 5,000 words to explain his doctrine.

In order to pass for more than their ability, the so-called honorable masters, professors, and experts (in America, especially) say little. They certainly have "mastered" the highest way of "oriental humility" and "secrecy," for it is definitely easier to look wise than to talk wisely. (To act wise is, of course, even more difficult.) The more they want to be taken at a value above their true worth, the more they will keep their mouths shut. For once they talk (or move), people can certainly classify and assess them accordingly.

I realize that the unknown is always wonderful and the "fifteenth-degree red-belt holders," the "experts from super-advanced schools," and the "honorable masters" know how to gather around themselves a mysterious veil of secrecy. However, keep in mind a Chinese saying that applies to these people: "Silence is the ornament and safeguard of the ignorant."

May it be well with you.

APPENDIX I

Bruce Lee's gung fu background at the time he wrote this book (c. 1959–1964)

1. *Wing Chun*: The only Chinese martial art that Bruce Lee truly studied in an in-depth and formal fashion for a prolonged period of time (five years). He learned the art from renowned master Yip Man.

2. *Tai chi ch'uan*: Lee learned the fundamentals of this art and remained quite taken with its central philosophy throughout his life. There is considerable indication that he learned the fundamentals from his father, although it is by no means clear which style of t'ai chi ch'uan Lee learned, for while his father studied the Wu style, Lee has been photographed performing movements from the yang style, and demonstrated the Yang Long form's 108 movements on at least one occasion (to his first student in America, Jesse Glover).

3. *Hung-gar*: Lee first learned the fundamentals of Hung-gar gung fu in Hong Kong from a friend of his father, Lee Hoi Chuen.

4. *Chin-na*: the art of chin-na emphasizes joint and wrist locks. Lee was familiar with aspects of this art, but there is no indication that he studied it formally.

Classical gung fu forms that Bruce Lee learned and/or demonstrated

1. Praying mantis
2. Southern mantis (this was the form he used most often during gung fu demonstrations in Seattle)
3. Wing Chun gung fu's sil lum tao
4. Jeet kune
5. Fu jow (tiger-claw) gung fu
6. Crane

The Tao of Gung Fu

Gung fu styles that held Bruce Lee's interest in the early 1960s

1. Tai chi
2. Northern praying mantis
3. Eagle claw
4. Pa-kua
5. Monkey boxing
6. Jeet kune
7. Choy Lay Fut

Gung fu styles that Bruce Lee read up on

(Mostly from bookstores located in Vancouver, Canada)

1. Southern mantis
2. Eagle claw
3. Dragon fist
4. T'ai chi ch'uan
5. Choy Lay Fut
6. Hsing-I
7. sil lum tao
8. Pa-kua
9. Hung-gar
10. Chin-na
11. Dim mak

(*Note:* Bruce Lee engaged in such study, according to both Taky Kimura and Seattle students Ed Hart, Jesse Glover, and Doug Palmer, because he wanted—even at this early stage—to create a superior gung fu system .)

APPENDIX II

Gung fu terminology

Sifu	Instructor
Sihing	Your senior, your older brother
Sidai	Your junior, your younger brother.
Sijo	Founder of the style and system
Sibak	Instructor's senior
Sisook	Instructor's junior
Sigung	Grandfather, your instructor's instructor
Todai	Student
Toshoon	Student's student (grandchildren)
Gwoon	School, gym (institute)
Jee yau bok gik	Freestyle sparring

1. Low hit—Ha da
2. Middle hit—Jun da
3. High hit—Go da

1. Straight kick—Jik tek
2. Side kick—Juk tek
3. Hook kick—O'ou tek
4. Rear kick—Hou tek

1. Finger jab—Biu jee
2. Straight blast—Jik chung
3. Vertical fist—Ch'ung chuie
4. Backfist—Gua chuie
5. Slapping hand—Pak sao
6. Grabbing hand—Lop sao
7. Jerking hand—Jut sao
8. Knuckle fist—Chop choy
9. Hooking fist—O'ou chuie
10. Horizontal fist—Ping chuie
11. Centerline—Jung Seen choy
12. Arm resting on opponents with hit—Fook da

APPENDIX III

Letters and gung fu scrapbook

Dear Bill,

    I am sorry to inform you that the articles have to be delayed because I am at present on a tour demonstrating Gung Fu. I've just got back from Los Angeles not too long ago and I'll have to start again in San Francisco. In a week or so I'll have to fly to New York.

    However, I'll try to find time in between to finish the article. By the way, there should be a coverage of the last tournament at Long Beach, and when will the next Black Belt be out?

    For your information the symbol in the zeal of the Jun Fan Gung Fu Institute is the symbol of Yin and Yang in which the Yin & Yang (black [passive] & white [active]) are two interlocking

of one WHOLE, each containing within

its confines the qualities of its complementaries (not opposite!) Instead of mutually exclusive, they are mutually dependent and are a function each of the other. When I say the heat makes me perspire the heat and perspiring are just "one" process as they are co-existent and the one could not exist but for the other. Just as an object need a subject, the person in attack is not taking an independent position but is acting as an assistant. After all, you need your opponent to complete the other half of a whole.

Thus gentleness/firmness is one inseparable force of one unceasing interplay of movement. If a person riding a bicycle wishes to go somewhere, he cannot pump on both the pedals at the same time or not pumping on them at all. In order to move forward he has to pump on one pedal and release the other. So the movement of going forward requires this "oneness" of pumping and releasing. Pumping is the result of releasing, and vice versa, each being the cause of the other.

This "oneness" is just a basic idea in the symbol then there are moderation without going to either extremes, the wonder of the ordinary — — — — —

In general, however, the idea is that _____ if Gung Fu is ~~extraordinary~~ extraordinary, it is because of the fact that it is nothing at all special — it is simply the direct expression of one's feeling with the minimum of lines and energy. The closer to the true Way; the less wastage of expression. there is

Please pardon my incoherence and poor penmanship.

Bruce Lee

GUNG FU

Gung Fu Forms

拳式一

The Turning Kick by Master Ng.

The golden Cock is a straight kick to groin

毒蛇攔蹄

伏牛昇心拳

Straight heart punch

The back fist 崩捶

鳥雞拜翼

crow style

白馬揚蹄一

Right flying front kick

Eagle claw with arm breaking technique

猛虎伸腰

陰輝捶

knuckle Fist to ribs

Tiger claw in Bow & Arrow Stance

Double Flying Kick

Gung Fu Training

彈箭拳双

Leg Training

Form Training

The Praying Mantis School (northern)
螳螂派 (北派)

The rib punch in bow & arrow stance

Prof. Law in a rib punch technique

"Two swallows fly through the forest" is a technique against three or more opponents.

The back fist to temple in Horse stance

The twisting straight kick to groin counter to a kidney punch

The Praying Mantis Stance

For attack from behind. Turning finger jab and low slant kick to shin

The Praying Mantis Hand

Praying Mantis, hand with finger thrust & straight groin kick combination

Foot sweep with hand stroke

The back of the hand to the face. Note the other hand that use to hook away the opponents guard.

Prof. Law with student mr. Wong Hin Fun.

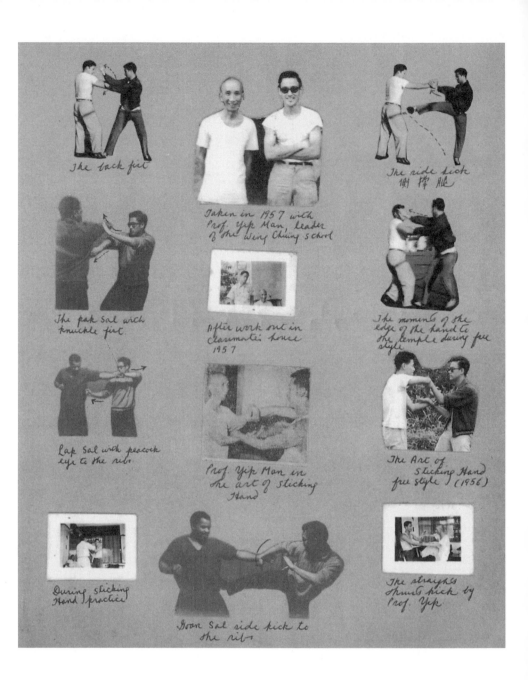

The back fist

Taken in 1957 with
Prof. Yip Man, leader
of the Weng Chung school

The side kick
側撐腿

The pak Sai with
knuckle fist

After work out in
classmates house
1957

The moments of the
edge of the hand to
the temple during free
style

Lap Sai with peacock
eye to the ribs

Prof. Yip Man in
the art of sticking
Hand

The Art of
Sticking Hand
free style (1956)

During sticking
Hand practice

Boan Sai side kick to
the ribs

The straight
thrust kick by
Prof. Yip.

The Eagle Claw School 鷹爪功

The Eagle Claw

The Hook

Straight thrust prick
with finger goto eyes

The Eagle Claw

The Eagle Claw
A
&
B

The wrist struke
after from the "hooking"
position

The single flying
kick

Edge of hand to
throat.

The one knuckle strike
to the solar plexus

The beak of the crane
and the picture below
are block.

The flying crane is
a heart thrust kick

The "Crane's beak" is a
blinding technique

"The Crane picking its food"
is an attack to the groin

"The Crane spreading its
wings" is an attack to
the groin

ABOUT THE AUTHORS

Bruce Lee (1940–1973) is generally considered the greatest martial artist of the twentieth century. A true Renaissance man, Lee was a talented artist, poet, philosopher, writer, and actor, apart from being a formidable fighter. His insights into philosophy physical fitness, self-defense, and moviemaking, have been enjoyed and lauded by millions of people around the world for well over two decades. He is the founder of jeet kune do, the first martial art to ever be predicated on total freedom for the individual practitioner. A learned man, Lee attended the University of Washington where he majored in philosophy. His personal library contains over 2,500 books on topics ranging from Eastern yoga to Western psychoanalysis. His achievements and example continue to inspire athletes and artists from around the world.

John Little is considered one of the world's foremost authorities on Bruce Lee, his training methods, and philosophies. Little is one of only a very few people to have ever been authorized to review the entirety of Lee's personal notes, sketches, and reading annotations. He is the former associate publisher of *Bruce Lee* magazine and former managing editor of *Knowing Is Not Enough: The Official Newsletter of Jun Fan Jeet Kune Do*. Little's expertise ranges from bodybuilding and martial arts to history and philosophy. He is the creator of the revolutionary Max Contraction Training strength training method. Little is the author of *The Warrior Within: The Philosophies of Bruce Lee* and *Max Contraction Training*, and the coauthor of *Body by Science, Power Factor Training, Static Contraction Training*, and dozens of other books. He has worked alongside some of the biggest names in bodybuilding, including Arnold Schwarzenegger, Lou Ferrigno, Mike Mentzer, and Steve Reeves. As a columnist, his articles on health and fitness have been published in such magazines as *Ironman, Muscle and Fitness, Flex, Men's Fitness, Inside Kung Fu*, and *Black Belt*.

TO THE READER

The Tuttle Publishing Bruce Lee Library Series is produced in association with the Bruce Lee Foundation, a 501(c)(3) Public Charity based in Los Angeles, California.

The Bruce Lee Foundation is the only not-for-profit organization dedicated to sharing Bruce Lee's insights with the world, by creating opportunities for individuals and applying his message as a personal call to action. They envision a world where Bruce Lee's message and the actions of the Bruce Lee Foundation inspire people to embrace their uniqueness and discover their limitless potential.

A portion of proceeds derived from the sale of this book will directly benefit the Bruce Lee Foundation, its programs and the individuals its programs support.

Get Involved:

www.bruceleefoundation.org
www.facebook.com/BruceLeeFoundation
www.twitter.com/BruceLeeFDN
www.instagram.com/BruceLeeFoundation

Contact:

Bruce Lee Foundation
11693 San Vicente Blvd, Ste 918
Los Angeles, CA 90049, USA
info@bruceleefoundation.com